# SPEAK TO ME

# SPEAK TO ME

## GREAT AMERICAN TEXTS DEMYSTIFIED
## FOR TODAY'S TEXT-MESSAGING STUDENTS

**BY RANDY HOWE**

Editorial Director: Jennifer Farthing
Senior Editor: Ruth Baygell
Production Editor: Caitlin Ostrow
Production Artist: Todd Bowman
Illustrator: Matt Morris
Cover and Interior Designer: Carly Schnur

Published by Kaplan Publishing, a division of Kaplan, Inc.
888 Seventh Ave.
New York, NY 10106

February 2007
10 9 8 7 6 5 4 3 2 1

ISBN-13: 978-1-4195-9549-3
ISBN-10: 1-4195-9549-0

Kaplan Publishing books are available at special quantity discounts to use for sales promotions, employee premiums, or educational purposes. Please call our Special Sales Department to order or for more information at 800-621-9621, ext. 4444, e-mail kaplanpubsales@kaplan.com, or write to Kaplan Publishing, 30 South Wacker Drive, Suite 2500, Chicago, IL 60606-7481.

# ABOUT THE AUTHOR

Randy Howe is the author of several books, including *Flags of the Fifty States and Their Incredible Histories*, *101 Ways to Adjust to High School*, *Word Source: The Smarter Way to Learn Vocabulary*, and *Training Wheels for Teachers*. He lives in Connecticut with his wife and two children and is a teacher in New Haven.

The author would like to thank everyone at Kaplan Publishing, especially Ruth Baygell, Caitlin Ostrow, Jennifer Farthing, and Maureen McMahon.

He would also like to acknowledge the social studies teachers at Fox Lane High School and the Political Science department at Hobart College.

This book is dedicated to Kevin Kuebler, the smartest kid on skates.

# TABLE OF CONTENTS

# INTRODUCTION

When a story is demystified, be it an urban legend or a rumor that has spread around your school faster than the flu, the truth is finally able to come out. All of a sudden you understand what was being said and why. When something is demystified, it is revealed *and* explained. No questions linger. A place of understanding has been reached.

Believe it or not, the things you study in school can be demystified just as easily as any tidbit of senseless gossip. Important documents from our nation's past can be demystified just as easily as the myth that eating celery can result in negative calories!

It is easier for you and your friends to find out the truth because unlike generations of the past, there is so much more information available to you. And when somebody learns something new, be it the truth about a rumor or the meaning of a speech written 200 years ago, that information can be shared faster than at any time in the past. Telephones used to be connected to walls and wires. These days, phones go where you can, no need to call: you can just text message the latest news to your family and friends.

Whether or not you text message, you're a part of a generation that's very different from other generations. The founding fathers (those men who guided our country from independence to the creation of the Constitution) didn't have phones nor did they have the Internet.

They wrote by dipping the tip of a quill into a jar of ink—not exactly what you'd call high-speed! The soldiers who fought in the Civil War's Battle of Gettysburg never once saw a reality show because TV was still 80-plus years away. The nurses who tended these men in the field hospitals weren't allowed to vote because they were women. The times certainly have changed and, for the most part, they have changed for the better.

The times have changed, but the people whose writings are included in this book weren't that different from you and your friends. Thomas Jefferson relied on his friends for help. Mark Twain liked to have fun. Sojourner Truth wanted respect. Abraham Lincoln preferred peace to war. John F. Kennedy was competitive and hoped to achieve great things. None of them could have ever predicted that their writing would be remembered for hundreds of years. If this were to happen to a story you wrote, you'd be just as surprised as Upton Sinclair when his novel, *The Jungle*, improved the quality of the food that our country produces. If this were to happen to a poem you wrote, you would be just as surprised as Francis Scott Key when his poem, "The Star-Spangled Banner," became our national anthem.

From *The Mayflower Compact* to Ronald Reagan's remarks at the Brandenburg Gate, there is a total of 16 historical documents in

*Speak to Me: Great American Texts Demystified for Today's Text-Messaging Students.* Though they aren't the only important texts ever written in the history of the United States, they are truly representative of the different eras of our history. From establishing colonies to fighting a revolution to protecting democracy and individual rights, the historical documents contained within say a lot about how far we have come as a country. They say a lot about the difference an individual can make when he or she decides to pick up a quill or sit down at a keyboard.

# HOW TO USE THIS BOOK

When the founding fathers gathered in Philadelphia to draw up *The Declaration of Independence,* and to create a plan for going to war against the British, there were hours of discussion and debate. When the editors at Kaplan gathered in New York City to create a plan for putting this book together, the same thing happened. There was debate and discussion, discussion and debate! What documents should be included? How should the information be presented so that this book is better than the typical textbook? Who should write such a book?

Well, I'm happy to say that they asked me to write it and although I may not be Thomas Jefferson, I do teach teenagers and I do know my history. So after some discussing and some debating of our own, the editor (a very nice, very smart woman named Ruth) and I decided on the layout for the book. The actual historical text can be seen in a blue box. Within the historical text, you'll find that some of the more difficult words are accompanied by a synonym in parentheses and written in blue. For example, this is the 2nd Amendment to *The Constitution of the United States of America:* "A well-regulated militia, being necessary to the security of a free State, the right of the people to keep and bear Arms (have weapons), shall not be infringed." The hope is that including a definition, or just a synonym, will make it easier to understand the language, because just as our country has changed, so has the English that we speak. Many of these texts were written before your grandmother's grandmother's grandmother was born, after all!

You will also notice that within the historical texts, there are some phrases that have been highlighted with bold text. These are key details and deserve extra attention, as they will really clue you in to the theme of the text. Pay close attention to the bold words, as well as those synonyms written in blue, and you'll have a pretty good understanding of what right each amendment to the Constitution protects, what James Monroe was really telling the world's other super powers in his Monroe Doctrine, what Mark Twain was saying about slavery and our nation's hypocrisy, and what John F. Kennedy was thinking about on the day that he became our 35th president. The process of demystifying our nation's history will be underway!

Before you begin reading the historical text, look for the summary under the heading "In 50 Words or Less." It's a short synopsis of what the text is all about. Later in the chapter, you will then find a longer summary that expands on the main theme of the text. I think it's important to shed some light on what was written and, even more importantly, why. And just as it helps to know who started the rumor, my students find it extremely helpful to know a little bit about the author when reading historical texts. Without the author there would be no document to consider and our nation's history might be very, very different. There might not be equal rights for men and women. There might not be equal access to education for all kids. There might not be an Internet or cell phones or MTV!

Similar to the "In 50 Words or Less" section, you'll find other important information under headings like "In Addition . . . ," "In Other Words," and "Who Would Write It Today?" These are all meant to not only teach you more about the historical document, but to make it more *memorable*. If you're able to make some sort of connection to the text, to the person who wrote the text, or to the reason why the text was written, you stand a much better chance of remembering it. And this is the point of our book: helping you to remember why each of these documents was written, as well as the impact it made on our nation's history.

Don't let the demystifying end with this book, either. When you're finished reading, the fun has actually just begun! If you learned something interesting, you can share it with a friend or somebody in your family. You can do an online search to find out even more. Originally, we were going to explore just 12 historical texts, but that number quickly rose to 16. This means there was limited space for describing each, so you need to become the researcher. Otherwise, there will be more myth and mystery left undiscovered. Read, research, and tell everyone you know about our nation's history. Teach them one fact about each of these important documents. You'll be happy you did and so will they!

# THE MAYFLOWER COMPACT

## NOVEMBER 1620

**In 50 Words or Less!** Before landing at Plymouth Rock, 41 men gathered on the Mayflower to sign the Mayflower Compact. This was their way of creating, and trying to maintain, a civilized society. Historians often describe the Mayflower Compact as the first American "constitution" because it established a government for the Pilgrims.

# THE MAYFLOWER COMPACT

In the name of God, Amen. We, whose names are underwritten, the Loyal Subjects **(citizens)** of our dread Sovereign Lord, King James, by the Grace of God, of Great Britain, France, and Ireland, King, Defender of the Faith, c.

Having undertaken for the Glory of God, and Advancement of the Christian Faith, and the Honour of our King and Country, a Voyage to plant the first colony **(settlement)** in the Northern Parts of Virginia; do, by these Presents, solemnly and mutually in the Presence of God and one of another, covenant **(agree)** and combine ourselves together into a civil Body Politic, for our better Ordering and Preservation, and Furtherance of the Ends aforesaid; **And by Virtue hereof do enact, constitute, and frame, such just and equal Laws, Ordinances, Acts, Constitutions, and Offices, from time to time, as shall be thought most meet and convenient for the General Good of the Colony;** unto which we promise all due Submission and Obedience.

In Witness whereof we have hereunto subscribed our names at Cape Cod the eleventh of November, in the Reign of our Sovereign Lord, King James of England, France, and Ireland, the eighteenth, and of Scotland, the fifty-fourth, Anno. Domini, 1620. ★

**SUMMARY:** In 1620, a group of men, women, and children began a journey across the Atlantic Ocean—a journey that included severe storms and no bathrooms or refrigerators—in the hopes of starting a new life in a new world. The Pilgrims wanted religious freedom, but they also wanted to survive. In order to do so, on the morning of November 11, 1620, 41 men aboard the Mayflower met to decide on a compact, or agreement, about how their colony would be governed. (As was customary at the time, only the men participated in this decision.) It is believed that William Bradford wrote the original draft of the Mayflower Compact which made clear that each Pilgrim would have to be responsible for himself, for his family, and also for each of his neighbors. All 41 men signed.

When a group of students gathers to start a project for school, at least one person in the group fears that he or she will get stuck doing all the work. The Pilgrims worried about this, too; nobody wanted to have to do all of the work, and nobody wanted a lazy person to benefit from their long hours of labor. They expected each Pilgrim to carry his or her weight, and the signers of the Mayflower Compact hoped that all of their fellow Pilgrims would work hard and also treat one another with respect. They knew that unless every Pilgrim cooperated, the colony would fail. And if the Plymouth Colony failed, it meant death for some if not all of the Pilgrims.

It is this kind of declaration of responsibility that makes the Mayflower Compact so memorable. It was the first in a long line of historical texts that added to the culture of our country. The Mayflower Compact was an easy choice for this book not only because it was the first form of a constitution in America, but also because it says a lot about what we expect from one another as fellow citizens.

To be specific, the Mayflower Compact made the government of the Plymouth Colony legitimate. Credit must be given to this document for getting the Pilgrims off on the right foot when that foot—those feet, to be exact!—landed on Plymouth Rock. Timber was cut, buildings were built, crops were planted, and Native Americans were greeted. Soon thereafter, other colonies sprung up in the New World and many of them used the Mayflower Compact as a model when establishing their own set of laws. It was the ruling document of the Plymouth Colony for 10 years and is still an important part of our history almost 400 years later.

Of course, the Pilgrims didn't get everything right. They'd meant to land in northern Virginia and ended up in Massachusetts instead, but we can cut them a break with their geography because their knowledge of human nature proved to be right on.

Their notion of the "civil Body Politic" is still a part of American culture today. Some think of it as the Golden Rule while others call it common decency. Thomas Paine might even call it common sense! It's the idea of treating others the same way that we hope they would treat us. Even more so, it's putting down in words the idea that "Laws, Ordinances, Acts, Constitutions, and Offices" will be established for the good of the town. As we all know, sometimes the Golden Rule isn't enough to make people behave decently toward one another. Rules must be established and enforced. Long before *COPS* and *America's Most Wanted*, the Pilgrims understood this. ★

**In Addition** . . . The Pilgrims aboard the Mayflower had reason to worry about their survival. Despite being very disciplined people—they were Puritans who lived their lives according to teachings of The Bible—they were aware of the disaster of an earlier colony in Jamestown, Virginia, where only 60 of the original 214 settlers survived. As it turned out, almost half of the Pilgrims failed to see 1621, dying during that first winter in the New World.

# Who Would Write It Today?

The Mayflower Compact was one group's attempt to coexist peacefully while trying to make a better life for themselves. In recognizing that only disciplined team players would be able to survive the harsh conditions of America, this kind of document could be an important part of any number of reality shows on TV today. Picture members of one of the "tribes" from *Survivor* signing their names to a similar compact before beginning the game. Every organization has to be organized, with rules (for the group) and roles (for individuals), so perhaps it would be the participants of *Survivor* who would write the Mayflower Compact today. Unlike in 1620, both men and women would be allowed to sign.

INTRODUCTION TO

# THOMAS PAINE'S COMMON SENSE

## THIRD EDITION

### FEBRUARY 1776

**In 50 Words or Less!** In the introduction seen here, Thomas Paine stated that each of the readers of *Common Sense* is really the author. They were all going to write the book of the American Revolution together, he felt, just as they were going to create a democratic government together.

# INTRODUCTION TO THOMAS PAINE'S *COMMON SENSE*, THIRD EDITION

Perhaps the sentiments **(opinions)** contained in the following pages, are not YET sufficiently fashionable to procure them general favour; a long habit of not thinking a thing WRONG, gives it a superficial appearance of being RIGHT, and raises at first a formidable outcry in defense of custom **(tradition)**. But the tumult soon subsides. Time makes more converts than reason **(wisdom)**.

As a long and violent abuse of power, is generally the Means of calling the right of it in question (and in Matters too which might never have been thought of, had not the Sufferers been aggravated into the inquiry) and as the King of England hath undertaken in his OWN RIGHT, to support the Parliament in what he calls THEIRS, and as the good people of this country are grievously oppressed by the combination, they have an undoubted privilege to inquire into the pretensions **(self-importance)** of both, and equally to reject the usurpation **(seizure)** of either.

In the following sheets, the author hath studiously avoided every thing which is personal among ourselves. Compliments as well as censure **(criticism)** to individuals make no part thereof. The wise, and the worthy, need not the triumph of a pamphlet; and those whose sentiments are injudicious **(foolish)**, or unfriendly, will cease of themselves unless too much pains are bestowed upon their conversion.

**SUMMARY:** Though Paine asked readers to think more about what was written rather than the person who'd done the writing, it's worth taking a minute to learn his story.

Paine was born in England in 1737 and eventually migrated to the New World. He never attended college, dropping out of school before his 13th birthday, and had several jobs until he met Benjamin Franklin during a trip to Paris. That turned out to be Paine's big break, as Franklin recommended him to a few of his publishing friends back in Philadelphia. Faster than an *American Idol* winner can put out a single, his ideas were being published in pamphlets and books.

The third edition of *Common Sense* was released in February of 1776, five months before the signing of the Declaration of Independence. It was an immediate best seller as colonists picked up more than 150,000 copies by the time the 13 colonies had united themselves as the 13 states. Talk of a revolution had increased greatly, and Paine's words really struck a chord with everyone who had a bone to pick with King George.

**The cause of America is in a great measure the cause of all man-kind.** Many circumstances hath, and will arise, which are not local, but universal, and through which the principles of all Lovers of Mankind are affected, and in the Event of which, their Affections are interested. **The laying a Country desolate with Fire and Sword, declaring War against the natural rights of all Mankind, and extirpating (totally destroying) the Defenders thereof from the Face of the Earth, is the Concern of every Man to whom Nature hath given the Power of feeling; of which Class, regardless of Party Censure, is the AUTHOR.**

P.S. The Publication of this new Edition hath been delayed, with a View of taking notice (had it been necessary) of any Attempt to refute (prove false) the Doctrine of Independance: As no Answer hath yet appeared, it is now presumed that none will, the Time needful for getting such a Performance ready for the Public being considerably past.

**Who the Author of this Production is, is wholly unnecessary to the Public, as the Object for Attention is the DOCTRINE (a principle or belief) ITSELF, not the MAN.** Yet it may not be necessary to say, That he is unconnected with any Party, and under no sort of Influence public or private, but the influence of reason and principle. ★

In Addition . . . In addition to freedom from Great Britain, Paine argued for freedom for individuals. As early as 1775, he wrote about putting an end to slavery: "Certainly one may, with as much reason and decency, plead for murder, robbery, lewdness, and barbarity, as for slavery."

One of the attractive things about *Common Sense* is that Paine wrote it in a way that even uneducated people, such as himself, could understand. The book also had wide appeal throughout the colonies because it challenged the authority of King George. Even more so, however, it was the first document to request independence from the king and from Great Britain. Paine also poked fun at the idea of having a government ruled by a monarch (king) because monarchs don't really know what's going on, being as far removed from all of the people as they are. He wrote, "The state of a king shuts him from the world, yet the business of a king requires him to know it thoroughly . . . "

Paine hadn't included his name in the first two editions of *Common Sense* but decided to do so this time around. In his introduction, he made clear that the reader shouldn't focus on the identity of the author but rather on what's being said. That's because Paine felt that each of the readers was, in a way, the author. All liberty-loving, tea-partying, no-taxation-without-represen-tation-thinking people were writing a history book—their own!

Also, Paine wasn't seeking fame or fortune for himself. He wanted to help put an end to King George's rule over the colonies. And he got what he wanted. Today, *Common Sense* is considered one of the most important documents in the nation's history and certainly one of the most symbolic of the revolutionary era. ★

---

**What Others Have Said:** In 1870, the famous American lecturer Robert Ingersoll remembered Thomas Paine fondly with these words: "He had more brains than books; more sense than education; more courage than politeness; more strength than polish."

---

# Who Would Write It Today?

Thomas Paine might've been a dropout, but he knew how to use words to get people fired up! In fact, he was so successful that he's now considered one of the founding fathers of the United States. Michael Moore makes movies like Thomas Paine wrote books—full of insightful and incite-ful ideas—and therefore some people agree with him while others do not. For Thomas Paine, there were the pro-American colonists to agree with while the Tories chose to take sides with the king. Moore's movies stir up controversy by strongly addressing issues like corporate greed, government ignorance, gun control, and the health care industry. Given these films and the fact that he has also written several books, it would probably be Michael Moore who would write *Common Sense* today.

# THE DECLARATION OF INDEPENDENCE

**JULY 1776**

**In 50 Words or Less!** When the Continental Congress decided it was time for the colonies to unite against Great Britain, they figured they should probably let King George know why they were rebelling. Thomas Jefferson did so by composing a list of complaints sprinkled with some of the most memorable prose in American history.

# THE DECLARATION OF INDEPENDENCE

IN CONGRESS, July 4, 1776

The unanimous Declaration of the thirteen united States of America

When in the Course of human events, **it becomes necessary for one people to dissolve the political bands which have connected them with another,** and to assume, among the powers of the earth, the separate and equal station to which the Laws of Nature and of Nature's God entitle them, a decent respect to the opinions of mankind requires that they should declare the causes which impel **(force)** them to the separation.

**We hold these truths to be self-evident (obvious), that all men are created equal, that they are endowed by their Creator with certain unalienable Rights, that among these are Life, Liberty and the pursuit of Happiness.** —That to secure these rights, Governments are instituted among Men, deriving their just powers from the consent **(approval)** of the governed,—That whenever any Form of Government becomes destructive of these ends, it is the Right of the People to alter or to abolish it, and to institute new Government, laying its foundation on such principles and organizing its powers in such form, as to them shall seem most likely to effect their Safety and Happiness. Prudence **(caution)**, indeed, will dictate that Governments long established should not be changed for light and transient causes; and

**SUMMARY:** Between June 11 and June 28, 1776, the Founding Fathers of the United States met to decide on a number of matters, not the least of which was the letter they would all sign and send to King George III. Though there was an element of "he said, she said" to the arguing that had been taking place between the colonists and the king, this was no mere email to let King George know how hurtful his gossiping was. No, this was the first shot fired in a revolution against the most powerful king in the world. So, Thomas Jefferson and his friends took their time—more than two weeks, in fact—to compose a letter of just 1,339 words.

In that letter, these men made very clear what they were doing (revolting to gain their independence) and why; all of those sentences starting with the word *He* are accusations against

---

**What Others Have Said:** The documentary filmmaker Ken Burns once said of Thomas Jefferson, "Here is the man who distilled a century of Enlightenment thinking into one remarkable sentence that begins, 'We hold these truths to be self-evident, that all men are created equal.' He is the author of our political freedom."

---

accordingly all experience hath shown, that mankind are more disposed to suffer, while evils are sufferable, than to right themselves by abolishing the forms to which they are accustomed. But when a long train of abuses and usurpations **(seizures)**, pursuing invariably the same Object evinces a design to reduce them under absolute Despotism, it is their right, it is their duty, to throw off such Government, and to provide new Guards for their future security.—Such has been the patient sufferance of these Colonies; and such is now the necessity which constrains them to alter their former Systems of Government. **The history of the present King of Great Britain is a history of repeated injuries and usurpations, all having in direct object the establishment of an absolute Tyranny (cruelty) over these States.** To prove this, let Facts be submitted to a candid world.

He has refused his Assent to Laws, the most wholesome and necessary for the public good.

He has forbidden his Governors to pass Laws of immediate and pressing importance, unless suspended in their operation till his Assent **(agreement)** should be obtained; and when so suspended, he has utterly neglected to attend to them.

He has refused to pass other Laws for the accommodation of large districts of people, unless those people would relinquish **(give up)** the right of Representation in the Legislature, a right inestimable to them and formidable to tyrants only.

He has called together legislative bodies at places unusual, uncomfortable, and distant from the depository of their public Records, for the sole purpose of fatiguing **(tiring)** them into compliance with his measures.

He has dissolved Representative Houses repeatedly, for opposing with manly firmness his invasions on the rights of the people.

He has refused for a long time, after such dissolutions, to cause others to be elected; whereby the Legislative powers, incapable of Annihilation, have returned to the People at large for their exercise; the State remaining in the mean time exposed to all the dangers of invasion from without, and convulsions within.

He has endeavoured to prevent the population of these States; for that purpose obstructing **(blocking)** the Laws of Naturalization of Foreigners; refusing to pass others to encourage their migrations hither, and raising the conditions of new Appropriations of Lands.

He has obstructed the Administration of Justice, by refusing his Assent to Laws for establishing Judiciary powers.

He has made Judges dependent on his Will alone, for the tenure of their offices, and the amount and payment of their salaries.

He has erected a multitude of New Offices, and sent hither swarms of Officers to harass our people, and eat out their substance.

He has kept among us, in times of peace, Standing Armies without the Consent of our legislatures.

He has affected to render the Military independent of and superior to the Civil power.

He has combined with others to subject us to a jurisdiction foreign to our constitution, and unacknowledged by our laws; giving his Assent to their Acts of pretended Legislation:

For Quartering **(housing)** large bodies of armed troops among us:

For protecting them, by a mock Trial, from punishment for any Murders which they should commit on the Inhabitants of these States:

For cutting off our Trade with all parts of the world:

**For imposing Taxes on us without our Consent (agreement):**

For depriving us, in many cases, of the benefits of Trial by Jury:

For transporting us beyond Seas to be tried for pretended offences:

King George for what he'd done to the colonies and to the colonists who lived and worked there.

In arguing for liberty, Jefferson called the reasons for revolution not just the truth, but the "self-evident" truth. He was saying that everything mentioned in the Declaration of Independence— from what the colonists had decided to do to why they were doing these things—was obvious. Plain-as-day obvious!

Of course all people want to be free. Of course all people want to have a say in how they are governed and in who governs them (free elections!). "We hold these truths to be self-evident" is a world-famous phrase from the Declaration of Independence, but equally well known is "Life, Liberty and the pursuit of Happiness." Of course all people want to pursue happiness. Of course all people want liberty and life. ★

In Addition . . . Thomas Jefferson is credited with writing the Declaration of Independence, but Benjamin Franklin and John Adams should also get some credit. Like good English teachers, they edited Jefferson's words, improving an already impressive document that would soon be signed by each of the 56 representatives sent to the Continental Congress.

For abolishing the free System of English Laws in a neighbouring Province, establishing therein an Arbitrary **(illogical)** government, and enlarging its Boundaries so as to render it at once an example and fit instrument for introducing the same absolute rule into these Colonies:

For taking away our Charters, abolishing our most valuable Laws, and altering fundamentally the Forms of our Governments:

For suspending our own Legislatures, and declaring themselves invested with power to legislate for us in all cases whatsoever.

He has abdicated **(abandoned)** Government here, by declaring us out of his Protection and waging War against us.

He has plundered **(raided)** our seas, ravaged our Coasts, burnt our towns, and destroyed the lives of our people.

He is at this time transporting large Armies of foreign Mercenaries **(hired soldiers)** to compleat the works of death, desolation and tyranny, already begun with circumstances of Cruelty & perfidy **(betrayal)** scarcely parallelled in the most barbarous ages, and totally unworthy of the Head of a civilized nation.

He has constrained our fellow Citizens taken Captive on the high Seas to bear Arms against their Country, to become the executioners of their friends and Brethren **(family)**, or to fall themselves by their Hands.

He has excited domestic insurrections **(rebellions)** amongst us, and has endeavoured to bring on the inhabitants of our frontiers, the merciless Indian Savages, whose known rule of warfare, is an undistinguished destruction of all ages, sexes and conditions.

In every stage of these Oppressions We have Petitioned for Redress **(reimbursement)** in the most humble terms: Our repeated Petitions have been answered only by repeated injury. A Prince, whose character is thus marked by every act which may define a Tyrant, is unfit to be the ruler of a free People.

Nor have We been wanting in attention to our Brittish brethren. We have warned them from time to time of attempts by their legislature to extend an unwarrantable jurisdiction over us. We have reminded them of the circumstances of our emigration and settlement here. We have appealed to their native justice and magnanimity, and we have conjured them by the ties of our common kindred to disavow these usurpations, which, would inevitably interrupt our connections and correspondence. They too have been deaf to the voice of justice and of consanguinity **(brotherhood)**. **We must, therefore, acquiesce in the necessity, which denounces our Separation, and hold them, as we hold the rest of mankind, Enemies in War, in Peace Friends.**

We, therefore, the Representatives of the United States of America, in General Congress, Assembled, appealing to the Supreme

Judge of the world for the rectitude (decency) of our intentions, do, in the Name, and by the Authority of the good People of these Colonies, solemnly publish and declare, **That these United Colonies are, and of Right ought to be Free and Independent States;** that they are Absolved (released) from all Allegiance to the British Crown, and that all political connection between them and the State of Great Britain, is and ought to be totally dissolved; and that as Free and Independent States, they have full Power to levy War, conclude Peace, contract Alliances, establish Commerce, and to do all other Acts and Things which Independent States may of right do. And for the support of this Declaration, with a firm reliance on the protection of divine Providence, **we mutually pledge to each other our Lives, our Fortunes and our sacred Honor.** ★

— John Hancock
   (as president of the Congress, Hancock was the first to sign)

**Georgia:**        Button Gwinnett, Lyman Hall, George Walton

**North Carolina:**   William Hooper, Joseph Hewes, John Penn

**South Carolina:**   Edward Rutledge, Thomas Heyward, Jr., Thomas Lynch, Jr., Arthur Middleton

**Massachusetts:**   John Hancock

**Maryland:**      Samuel Chase, William Paca, Thomas Stone, Charles Carroll of Carrollton

| | |
|---|---|
| **Virginia:** | George Wythe, Richard Henry Lee, Thomas Jefferson, Benjamin Harrison, Thomas Nelson, Jr., Francis Lightfoot Lee, Carter Braxton |
| **Pennsylvania:** | Robert Morris, Benjamin Rush, Benjamin Franklin, John Morton, George Clymer, James Smith, George Taylor, James Wilson, George Ross |
| **Delaware:** | Caesar Rodney, George Read, Thomas McKean |
| **New York:** | William Floyd, Philip Livingston, Francis Lewis, Lewis Morris |
| **New Jersey:** | Richard Stockton, John Witherspoon, Francis Hopkinson, John Hart, Abraham Clark |
| **New Hampshire:** | Josiah Bartlett, William Whipple |
| **Massachusetts:** | Samuel Adams, John Adams, Robert Treat Paine, Elbridge Gerry |
| **Rhode Island:** | Stephen Hopkins, William Ellery |
| **Connecticut:** | Roger Sherman, Samuel Huntington, William Williams, Oliver Wolcott |
| **New Hampshire:** | Matthew Thornton |

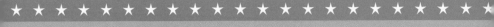

# Who Would Write It Today?

Thomas Jefferson was the brains behind the original Declaration of Independence. This time around, Bill Gates gets to do the writing and chances are the document would appear on a website rather than on parchment paper! Gates has revolutionized the world by making personal computers a part of everyday life for a vast majority of Americans just as the Founding Fathers revolutionized the world by promoting rule of the people by the people (aka democracy). So, perhaps it would be Bill Gates who would write the Declaration of Independence today.

# PREAMBLE TO THE U.S. CONSTITUTION

## SEPTEMBER 1787

**In 50 Words or Less!** Short and sweet, this is the introduction to the Constitution. While the Constitution is a set of rules for the federal government, the Preamble states what the Founding Fathers wanted to "establish," "insure," "provide," "promote," and "secure" with this document that has now been in existence for over 200 years.

# PREAMBLE TO THE U.S. CONSTITUTION

**We the People of the United States, in Order to form a more perfect Union,** establish Justice, insure domestic Tranquility **(calm),** provide for the common defence, promote the general Welfare, and secure the Blessings of Liberty to ourselves and our Posterity **(future generations), do ordain and establish this Constitution for the United States of America.** ★

**SUMMARY:** The Preamble to the U.S. Constitution is a declaration of incredible intentions. Think of it in terms your English teacher might use: It is the *main topic sentence* that the members of the Constitutional Convention included so that everyone who would ever read this document could be formally informed, right off the bat, as to what The Constitution is all about.

So it was, in 1787, that all of the state representatives agreed to "We the People" as the opening phrase. This might seem repetitive, but sometimes you have to say something twice to make sure you're heard, right? It was a man named Gouverneur Morris who wrote that famous opening line. He was the founding father in charge of the committee to write The Constitution. This group was known as the "Committee of Stile and Arrangement" and included Morris, James Madison, Alexander Hamilton, and a couple of other old white guys in wigs. Incredibly though, Morris was just 35 when he was charged with leading the effort to review and rewrite the articles, laws, and assorted documents that would soon constitute our constitution.

Morris liked "We the people" but he loved his follow-up phrase, "in Order to form a more perfect Union." This statement left no doubt that The Constitution was America taking its shot at creating the greatest government the world had ever known. And how about that? Morris succeeded just as America has succeeded. ★

In Addition . . . The Preamble was also meant to help Americans move past the Articles of Confederation, which was our first national constitution. The Articles of Confederation did more to preserve the independence of each individual state than to establish a strong federal government and this might be why the phrase "to form a more perfect Union" appears in the Preamble to the U.S. Constitution. After all, it's the federal government that united all of the states.

# Who Would Write It Today?

Timbaland might produce an album, and the artist—be it Missy Elliott, Nelly Furtado, or Bubba Sparxxx—might ask him to do a little intro before the music kicks in. Timbaland, like the Founding Fathers, could lay out for the listener why he or she didn't waste their money buying the song and why the collaboration is sure to impress. Can't you just hear it? "We the people at Beat Club Records . . . ." So perhaps it would be Timbaland who would write the Preamble today.

# THE
# BILL OF RIGHTS

**SEPTEMBER 1789
RATIFIED DECEMBER 1791**

**In 50 Words or Less!** The Preamble began the Constitution, and the Bill of Rights ended it. Not only did these first 10 amendments guarantee individual rights, they ensured that each of the 13 states would ratify the Constitution. Without the Bill of Rights, the longest-lasting constitution in the world might never have been approved.

# THE BILL OF RIGHTS

The Ten Original Amendments to the Constitution of the United States
Passed by Congress September 25, 1789
Ratified December 15, 1791

*Amendment I*
Congress shall make no law respecting an establishment of religion,
or prohibiting the free exercise thereof; or abridging **(reducing)**
**the freedom of speech, or of the press;** or the right of the people
peaceably to assemble, and to petition the Government for a redress
**(remedy)** of grievances.

*Amendment II*
A well-regulated Militia, being necessary to the security of a free State,
**the right of the people to keep and bear Arms (have weapons),**
shall not be infringed.

*Amendment III*
No Soldier shall, in time of peace be quartered **(live)** in any house,
**without the consent of the Owner,** nor in time of war, but in a
manner to be prescribed by law.

**SUMMARY:** Two hundred–plus years after being written, the U.S. Constitution is still used today as a guide for our federal government. It is referred to by the president, by Congress, and by the Supreme Court just as it is referred to by other countries hoping to create a democracy of their own.

In fact, the Constitution is so well respected that it was actually an American—General Douglas MacArthur—who helped Japan revise its constitution following its defeat in World War II. The beginning of the Japanese Constitution should sound very familiar: "We, the Japanese people . . . ." A number of countries have tried to duplicate our governmental framework—some have been successful, some have not—but at this point the U.S. Constitution is the longest-existing constitution in the world.

One of the reasons the Constitution is still in existence is that it's a flexible document; it can change with the times. With the ability to add amendments, the Constitution continues to be relevant and useful today.

Amendments are meant to improve the Constitution, and the Bill of Rights did just that by ensuring individual rights. In the years following the American Revolution, citizens were

*Amendment IV*
The right of the people to be secure in their persons, houses, papers, and effects, **against unreasonable searches and seizures,** shall not be violated, and no Warrants shall issue, but upon probable cause, supported by oath or affirmation, and particularly describing the place to be searched, and the persons or things to be seized.

*Amendment V*
No person shall be held to answer for a capital, or otherwise infamous crime, unless on a presentment or indictment (accusation) of a Grand Jury, except in cases arising in the land or naval forces, or in the Militia, when in actual service in time of War or public danger; **nor shall any person be subject for the same offense to be twice put in jeopardy (danger) of life or limb;** nor shall be compelled in any criminal case to be a witness against himself, nor be deprived of life, liberty, or property, without due process of law; nor shall private property be taken for public use without just compensation.

*Amendment VI*
In all criminal prosecutions, **the accused shall enjoy the right to a speedy and public trial,** by an impartial jury of the State and district wherein the crime shall have been committed, which district shall have been previously ascertained by law, and to be informed of the nature and cause of the accusation; to be confronted with the witnesses against him; to have compulsory process for obtaining witnesses in his favor, and to have the Assistance of Counsel for his defence.

still worried about protecting their rights, as were each of the states. Rhode Island was the last to ratify (accept) the Constitution—it finally signed in 1791—and, like some of the other states, worried that the president would try to rule like a king. Rhode Island wanted to limit the rights of the federal government just as the individual citizens did.

So, the Bill of Rights was created and tacked on to the end of the Constitution. Here is a summary of the 10 amendments that it contains.

*Amendment 1:*
Freedom of religion and speech; also, the freedom to gather for a meeting as long as it's done peacefully.

*Amendment 2:*
The right to bear arms; there are specific laws now to outline what kinds of weapons people can and cannot have.

*Amendment 3:*
The government can't force citizens to house and feed soldiers.

*Amendment 4:*
Law enforcement officials can only search your house, and take your stuff, if they have a warrant.

*Amendment VII*

In Suits at common law, where the value in controversy shall exceed twenty dollars, **the right of trial by jury shall be preserved,** and no fact tried by a jury shall be otherwise re-examined in any Court of the United States, than according to the rules of the common law.

*Amendment VIII*

Excessive **(unnecessarily high)** bail shall not be required, nor excessive fines imposed, **nor cruel and unusual punishments inflicted.**

*Amendment IX*

The enumeration **(details)** in the Constitution, of certain rights, shall not be construed to deny or disparage others retained by the people.

*Amendment X*

The powers not delegated to the United States by the Constitution, nor prohibited by it to the States, are reserved **(given)** to the States respectively, or to the people. ★

*Amendment 5:*

When accused of a capital offense, an official charge has to come from a Grand Jury; also, a person cannot be tried twice for the same crime.

*Amendment 6:*

The accused have a right to a speedy trial by a jury that lives in the area where the crime was committed; also, the accused has the right to a defense attorney even if the individual cannot afford one.

*Amendment 7:*

When a lawsuit involves money or objects worth more than $20, a jury and not a judge will decide.

---

**In Addition** . . . Many more amendments have been added to the Constitution since the Bill of Rights. For example, the 26th Amendment, passed in 1970, lowered the voting age for all federal, state, and local elections to 18 years of age. Before this, the voting age was 21 even though all male citizens had to register for the military draft at 18.

---

*Amendment 8:*
Unnecessarily expensive bail, or fines, cannot be required and unnecessarily cruel punishments cannot be forced on those who are found guilty.

*Amendment 9:*
The rights given in the Constitution can't be used to deny other rights already given to the citizens.

*Amendment 10:*
The same is true of the states; also, any rights of the federal government not mentioned specifically in the Constitution automatically belong to the states. ★

---

In Addition . . . Both houses of Congress vote whether or not to add an amendment to the Constitution. Interestingly enough, the amendment is then passed to the states to vote their approval and not to the president as you might expect.

---

# Who Would Write It Today?

Burger King® has long told you that you can "Have it your way!" and this kind of individualized service is similar to the spirit of the Bill of Rights. If you like mustard rather than ketchup, then the Burger King is going to give you a burger with mustard and no ketchup. If you don't like ice in your soda, no problem. You serve yourself at the soda bar. Also, it's important to note that this is the case at Burger King locations all across the country. Go anywhere in the United States and you can enjoy the rights provided by the Bill of Rights just like you can "Have it your way!" So, if he were to lay down the spatula for a minute and pick up a pen, perhaps it would be the Burger King who would write the Bill of Rights today!

# MARBURY V. MADISON

**FEBRUARY 1803**

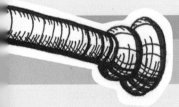

**In 50 Words or Less!** While in office, George Washington defined the role of president for future presidents. Ten years later, it was the *Marbury v. Madison* decision, written by the chief justice of the Supreme Court, John Marshall, that defined the role of the court in our system of checks and balances.

# EXCERPT FROM *MARBURY V. MADISON*

It is emphatically **(definitely)** the province and **duty of the judicial department to say what the law is.** Those who apply the rule to particular cases, must of necessity expound **(explain)** and interpret that rule. If two laws conflict with each other, the courts must decide on the operation of each. So if a law be in opposition to the constitution: if both the law and the constitution apply to a particular case, so that the court must either decide that case conformably to the law, disregarding the constitution; or conformably to the constitution, disregarding the law: the court must determine which of these conflicting rules governs the case. This is of the very essence **(spirit)** of judicial duty.

If then the courts are to regard the constitution; and the constitution is superior to any ordinary act of the legislature; **the constitution, and not such ordinary act, must govern the case to which they both apply.** Those then who controvert **(negate)** the principle that the constitution is to be considered, in court, as a paramount law, are reduced to the necessity of maintaining that courts must close their eyes on the constitution, and see only the law. This doctrine would subvert **(weaken)** the very foundation of all written constitutions. ★

**SUMMARY:** On the opposite page is an excerpt from the first *really* important decision that the Supreme Court ever made. The full name of the case is *William Marbury v. James Madison, Secretary of State of the United States,* and the majority opinion was written by Chief Justice John Marshall. The case was decided in 1803, a month after Thomas Jefferson was inaugurated as president and 27 years after the United States became an independent nation. What made our country unique—besides the idea of a democratically elected government—was the system of checks and balances that had been outlined in the Constitution.

The Supreme Court, Congress, and the president are the three branches of government, and part of the job function of each branch is to keep the other two branches in "check." The three "balance" each other out by making sure that one doesn't have more power than the others. (Yes, the president seems to have more power but legally does not.) With the *Marbury v. Madison* decision, the Supreme Court established what its role would be within this system.

The excerpt included here was written by Marshall, and in it he used the oath to uphold the Constitution that the judges take as part of the justification for the Supreme Court's decision to overrule a law of Congress. He also used it as part of the justification for giving the Constitution priority over all other laws.

Now, the nitty gritty of what was going on: The two presidents before Jefferson—George Washington and John Adams—were both from the Federalist Party, and when they appointed judges, they appointed only those from their own party. The way that these appointments were made, the judges got the job for life. (Imagine if you were given your dream job and told it was yours for life, no matter how well or poorly you performed!)

The problem was, Thomas Jefferson was a Democratic-Republican— the opposition to the Federalist Party at that time—and in an obviously political move, he refused to deliver the appointments to the judges named by John Adams. One of these appointed judges, William Marbury, brought his case to the Supreme Court to fight this refusal. When it was time for the Supreme Court judges to make their decision, they felt like they were caught between a rock and a hard place: Marshall knew that if he tried to overturn Jefferson's decision, Jefferson, being the president and all, would just ignore him. If that happened, everyone would think of the Supreme Court as nothing more than a powerless joke.

So after much thought, Marshall wrote an opinion that criticized Jefferson and his secretary of state (James Madison) but supported their right *not* to deliver the appointments. He based this on the fact

In Addition . . . The ability to interpret the Constitution has allowed the Supreme Court, in recent years, to expand individual rights with court decisions, such as with *Brown v. Board of Education* (led to desegregation of schools), *Miranda v. Arizona* (police must inform those being arrested of their rights), and *Roe v. Wade* (a woman has a legal right to have an abortion).

that Article III of the Constitution took priority over the Judicial Act of 1789. This act was passed by Congress to empower the Supreme Court to order the delivery of court appointments; Marshall said not only that the court could overrule Congress, but also that the laws in the Constitution were *more* important than the law that had been passed by Congress and signed by the president. He wrote, "the constitution, and not such ordinary act, must govern the case to which they both apply."

Jefferson ultimately didn't complain because the court had said he could legally withhold those appointments and that was what he really cared about. Besides, as president, Jefferson really couldn't argue against this judicial reinforcement of the system of checks and balances. You'll notice that Marshall made his point by saying that the Supreme Court *couldn't* overrule Article III of the Constitution. He lost the battle to win the war, appearing to take power away from his court, but really giving it much more than it had before. The Supreme Court was now on equal ground with the other two branches of government and the sole interpreter of the Constitution.

Confusing? Yes.
Important? Definitely yes! ★

# Who Would Write It Today?

Just as Chief Justice Marshall established the Supreme Court's ability to interpret the Constitution, President George W. Bush tried to defeat terrorism by increasing his ability to act as Commander in Chief. He pushed the limits as to how prisoners of war can be held and questioned. He also approved the investigation of private phone records and other such information-finding methods that many Americans felt were unconstitutional.

Because it is the president's job to protect the people, Bush saw these actions as justified. So if someone were to write a modern version of the *Marbury v. Madison* decision, it would probably be President George W. Bush.

# "THE STAR-SPANGLED BANNER"

## SEPTEMBER 1814

**In 50 Words or Less!** "The Star-Spangled Banner" that Francis Scott Key wrote was actually a poem. A lawyer, Key was inspired by an American flag that he saw while being held captive by the British during the War of 1812. President Herbert Hoover made it the national anthem in 1931.

# "THE STAR-SPANGLED BANNER"

O say can you see, by the dawn's early light,
What so proudly we hail'd at the twilight's last gleaming,
Whose **broad stripes and bright stars** through the perilous fight
O'er the ramparts we watch'd, were so gallantly **(courageously)**
streaming?
And the rocket's red glare, the bombs bursting in air,
**Gave proof through the night that our flag was still there,**
O say does that star-spangled banner yet wave
O'er the land of the free and the home of the brave?

On the shore dimly seen through the mists of the deep,
Where the foe's haughty **(proud)** host in dread silence reposes,
What is that which the breeze, o'er the towering steep,
As it fitfully blows, half conceals, half discloses **(reveals)**?
Now it catches the gleam of the morning's first beam,
In full glory reflected now shines on the stream,
'Tis the star-spangled banner—O long may it wave
O'er the land of the free and the home of the brave!

And where is that band who so vauntingly swore **(promised)**,
That the havoc of war and the battle's confusion
A home and a Country should leave us no more?
Their blood has wash'd out their foul footstep's pollution.
No refuge could save the hireling and slave

**SUMMARY:** After defeating the British in the Revolutionary War, the United States of America didn't automatically become a world superpower. In fact, Great Britain still had great interest in the New World and its continued presence eventually led to another war, the War of 1812. Leading up to the war, the British were so bold as to capture American sailors and force them to work on British ships. Like an older brother who won't get out of your room, the British also had a habit of ordering their army and navy to hang out where we didn't necessarily want them to be.

We Americans didn't want to tell Mom and Dad, though. We wanted to *be* Mom and Dad! So the United States began a war that would last for two years and end in an eventual stalemate.

During the war, the British were able to invade the United States, including Washington, DC. The British were doing their best to burn the city to the ground, so Dolly Madison, the wife of President James Madison, began taking valuables from the White House in order to save them. The British were able to attack the capital because they controlled Chesapeake Bay. They also wanted to attack Baltimore; to do so, they had to gain control of Fort McHenry, which was at the mouth of Baltimore Harbor. Like all American forts, Fort McHenry flew several American flags and one of them would lead to the creation of our national anthem.

From the terror of flight or the gloom of the grave,
**And the star-spangled banner in triumph doth wave**
O'er the land of the free and the home of the brave.

O thus be it ever when freemen shall stand
Between their lov'd home and the war's desolation **(misery)**!
Blest with vict'ry and peace, may the heav'n rescued land
**Praise the power that hath made and preserv'd us a nation!**
Then conquer we must, when our cause it is just,
And this be our motto — "In God is our trust,"
And the star-spangled banner in triumph shall wave
O'er the land of the free and the home of the brave. ★

In Addition . . . "God Bless America" is a patriotic song that, like the national anthem, can be heard at baseball games. Currently, "The Star-Spangled Banner" is played before the first pitch while at many stadiums "God Bless America" is played during the seventh inning. This tradition began after the tragedies of 9/11.

The British attacked Fort McHenry in 1814 and while doing so, an American lawyer named Francis Scott Key was temporarily held captive by them. Contrary to the popular myth, Key was not an actual prisoner. He was on board the *HMS Tonnant* to secure the release of a doctor who was being held prisoner. (The captain dined with Key, who brought with him testimonials from British soldiers to whom the doctor had tended.) After dinner, the captain couldn't let Key return to land because, while they ate, he'd heard details of the planned attack on Fort McHenry. So Key was returned to the *HMS Minden* and there he stayed throughout the battle, which lasted for more than a day. It was during the battle that Key noticed an American flag, with its 15 stars and 15 stripes (in honor of the 15 states at the time), flying above the fort. Finding the sight so inspirational that it was still on his mind the following day, he wrote this now-famous poem upon his release.

"The Star-Spangled Banner" went from poem to song when it was set, amazingly enough, to a British tune called "To Anacreon in Heaven." Key's brother-in-law paid to have copies of the song printed, and soon newspapers all across the country were publishing it. Singers began to sing "The Star-Spangled Banner" and its popularity grew even more. The song was performed most often on the Fourth of July and, in 1916, President Woodrow Wilson ordered that it be played at military ceremonies. Two years later, the song made its first appearance at a baseball game when spontaneously played by a band during the World Series. In 1931, President Herbert Hoover signed a bill adopting "The Star-Spangled Banner" as the national anthem.

You will notice that the poem is 32 lines, four times as long as the song. To state the obvious, this was done so the song would have a more acceptable length. Though much of the song is more general in its patriotism, some of the lines are specific to what Key observed that night in 1814, such as "And the rocket's red glare, the bombs bursting in air, Gave proof through the night that our flag was still there . . . ." And if the flag was there, that meant that the Americans were still there, inside Fort McHenry and victorious over the British. Perhaps the song has lasted as our national anthem because of how much our country has survived in its history; because, unfortunately, there have been so many situations where if that flag had come down, it would've been an indicator that our soldiers had been defeated.

Key's words also put a vivid image into the reader's (or listener's) mind. You can practically see the flag way up high on its flagpole. When he wrote, "As it fitfully blows, half conceals, half discloses," he was painting the picture of the flag waving in the breeze and hinting at its full glory for all to see, enemy and ally alike. In the end, that flag disclosed, or revealed, that America would not fall under British control again. There was reason for celebration and continued patriotism.

At the conclusion of the War of 1812, feelings of nationalism were running high, because we had, once again, fought valiantly against the strongest military force in the world. America had earned the respect of other nations and was well on its way to becoming a superpower. It only makes sense that, like those other countries, we have a national anthem to express such feelings of patriotism. The only surprising thing is that it took so long to name a national anthem! ★

What Others Have Said: Several other patriotic songs are widely recognized by Americans. These include "America the Beautiful," "Yankee Doodle," "This Land Is Your Land," and another ode to the American flag, "You're a Grand Old Flag."

# Who Would Write It Today?

In 2006, Katie Couric became the first female anchor to deliver the evening news, solo, for a major network. In reporting on world events for CBS, she is also responsible for deciding which events are the most important for the public to learn about. When writing her script, she has to be very descriptive in as few words as possible. Couric is a spokeswoman for colon cancer awareness, and millions of people rely on her to be informed about important issues, such as natural disasters, elections, and wars. That is why, if "The Star-Spangled Banner" were to be written today, Katie Couric would probably be the one to write it.

# THE MONROE DOCTRINE

### DECEMBER 1823

In 50 Words or Less! The Monroe Doctrine was America's warning to the world that we would protect countries and territories in the Western Hemisphere from European colonization. The Monroe Doctrine was made public in 1823, during President James Monroe's annual speech to Congress, and is recognized today as our country's first foreign policy.

# EXCERPT FROM THE MONROE DOCTRINE

At the proposal of the Russian Imperial Government, made through the minister of the Emperor residing here, a full power and instructions have been transmitted to the minister of the United States at St. Petersburg to arrange by amicable **(friendly)** negotiation the respective rights and interests of the two nations on the northwest coast of this continent. A similar proposal has been made by His Imperial Majesty to the Government of Great Britain, which has likewise been acceded **(agreed)** to. The Government of the United States has been desirous by this friendly proceeding of manifesting the great value which they have invariably attached to the friendship of the Emperor and their solicitude to cultivate the best understanding with his Government. In the discussions to which this interest has given rise and in the arrangements by which they may terminate the occasion has been judged proper for asserting, **as a principle in which the rights and interests of the United States are involved, that the American continents, by the free and independent condition which they have assumed and maintain, are henceforth not to be considered as subjects for future colonization by any European powers.**

It was stated at the commencement **(beginning)** of the last session that a great effort was then making in Spain and Portugal to improve the condition of the people of those countries, and that it appeared to be conducted with extraordinary moderation. It need scarcely

**SUMMARY:** It's called the Monroe Doctrine, but if history were to give credit where credit's due, it would be known as "The Adams Doctrine." The reason for this is that John Quincy Adams, President James Monroe's secretary of state, actually came up with the protectionist ideas that Monroe presented to Congress in 1823. Score one for Monroe.

(Don't feel bad for JQA, though. Not only was he the son of President John Adams, he would go on to become president himself!)

According to Monroe's speech, Spain and Portugal had presented themselves as having the best of intentions, but in recent years their actions in their New World colonies had disappointed the U.S. government. He reminded these countries, "The citizens of the United States cherish sentiments the most friendly in favor of the liberty and happiness of their fellow-men on that side of the Atlantic." That being said, Monroe assured them that we weren't as concerned with existing colonies as we were with territories that held our interest and those new nations that had already established their independence.

One thing that allowed Monroe to make his declarations with such confidence was the knowledge that we weren't the be remarked that the results have been so far very different from what was then anticipated. Of events in that quarter of the globe, with which we have so much intercourse (communication) and from which we derive our origin, we have always been anxious and interested spectators. **The citizens of the United States cherish sentiments the most friendly in favor of the liberty and happiness of their fellow-men on that side of the Atlantic. In the wars of the European powers in matters relating to themselves we have never taken any part, nor does it comport with our policy to do so. It is only when our rights are invaded or seriously menaced that we resent (dislike) injuries or make preparation for our defense.** With the movements in this hemisphere we are of necessity more immediately connected, and by causes which must be obvious to all enlightened and impartial observers. The political system of the allied powers is essentially different in this respect from that of America. This difference proceeds from that which exists in their respective Governments; and to the defense of our own, which has been achieved by the loss of so much blood and treasure, and matured by the wisdom of their most enlightened (open-minded) citizens, and under which we have enjoyed unexampled felicity (great happiness), this whole nation is devoted. We owe it, therefore, to candor (honesty) and to the amicable relations existing between the United States and those powers **to declare that we should consider any attempt on their part to extend their system to any portion of this hemisphere as dangerous to our peace and safety.** With the existing colonies or dependencies of any European power only ones thinking these thoughts. There were other countries that wanted to keep Spain and Portugal in check (Russia and France, too). For example, the British shared our concern. Like us, they had no interest in seeing these nations, especially Spain, extend their control in the Western Hemisphere. So, we let bygones be bygones and welcomed Britain's world-class navy to the cause. Who could blame Monroe and Adams for burying the hatchet?

This was a huge help—like getting the code that finally helps you to beat a Batman video game—but Monroe and Adams didn't want the world to just see us as Britain's little sidekick. We needed to be considered more than Robin to their Batman. America had *earned* the right to be considered a superpower, and to simply go along with Britain's policy would be embarrassing. That is why Monroe decided to inform the world, via his address to Congress, of our new attitude. He told the Old World powers that if they tried to colonize any more territories in the Caribbean, Central America, or South America, the United States would have to get all up in their grill. Any threat and we'd come out fightin'!

But being the wise politician that he was, Monroe also offered a trade-off: he promised that the United States wouldn't interfere with any wars fought *between* the European superpowers. Of course, being a politician, this was an empty promise we have not interfered and shall not interfere. **But with the Governments who have declared their independence and maintained it, and whose independence we have, on great consideration and on just principles, acknowledged, we could not view any interposition for the purpose of oppressing them, or controlling in any other manner their destiny, by any European power in any other light than as the manifestation (expression) of an unfriendly disposition toward the United States.** In the war between those new Governments and Spain we declared our neutrality at the time of their recognition, and to this we have adhered, and shall continue to adhere, provided no change shall occur which, in the judgment of the competent authorities of this Government, shall make a corresponding change on the part of the United States indispensable (very important) to their security.

The late events in Spain and Portugal show that Europe is still unsettled. Of this important fact no stronger proof can be adduced than that the allied powers should have thought it proper, on any principle satisfactory to themselves, to have interposed (interfered) by force in the internal concerns of Spain. To what extent such interposition may be carried, on the same principle, is a question in which all independent powers whose governments differ from theirs are interested, even those most remote, and surely none of them more so than the United States. Our policy in regard to Europe, which was adopted at an early stage of the wars which have so long agitated that quarter of the globe, nevertheless remains the same, which is, not to

that we didn't keep for very long, and although the Monroe Doctrine is a memorable policy, we really only interfered with other country's efforts at colonization when it benefited us economically. But, a message had been sent: the United States had a foreign policy and other nations had better listen up. ★

In Addition . . . In 1898, the United States earned victory in the Spanish-American War, a war that was certainly fought with the Monroe Doctrine in mind. We gained control of Puerto Rico and Cuba as a result of the war and 64 years later, when the Soviet Union was exerting its influence, via communism, over Cuba, President John F. Kennedy said, "The Monroe Doctrine means what it has meant since President Monroe and John Quincy Adams enunciated it, and that is that we would oppose a foreign power extending its power to the Western Hemisphere, and that is why we oppose what is happening in Cuba today." He declared an end to trade with Cuba, and it hasn't resumed since that day.

interfere in the internal concerns of any of its powers; to consider the government de facto as the legitimate government for us; to cultivate friendly relations with it, and to preserve those relations by a frank, firm, and manly policy, meeting in all instances the just claims of every power, submitting to injuries from none. But in regard to those continents circumstances are eminently **(extremely)** and conspicuously different. **It is impossible that the allied powers should extend their political system to any portion of either continent without endangering our peace and happiness;** nor can anyone believe that our southern brethren, if left to themselves, would adopt it of their own accord. It is equally impossible, therefore, that we should behold such interposition in any form with indifference. If we look to the comparative strength and resources of Spain and those new Governments, and their distance from each other, it must be obvious that she can never subdue **(control)** them. It is still the true policy of the United States to leave the parties to themselves, in hope that other powers will pursue the same course. ★

In Addition . . . In 1845, President James Polk referred to the Monroe Doctrine when justifying our westward expansion. This was the beginning of a policy of his own, known as Manifest Destiny, in which Polk said it was our nation's destiny to occupy the territories west of the Mississippi River so that our country could grow and prosper. By expanding, he said, we would be protecting our interests, thus the reference to the Monroe Doctrine.

# Who Would Write It Today?

Over the years, Homer Simpson has had a number of problems with other characters on the popular show *The Simpsons*. Neighbor Ned Flanders intrudes so often that Homer wrote a song titled "Everybody Hates Ned Flanders." Montgomery Burns, Homer's boss, stole the Simpson's puppies! It's only natural then that Homer would want to keep people like Flanders and Burns out of his home. So, it would probably be Homer Simpson who would write the Monroe Doctrine today.

**NOTE:** Actually, it would be his brainy daughter, Lisa, who would write it. Homer would "borrow" her ideas, just like Monroe did with Adams. D'oh!

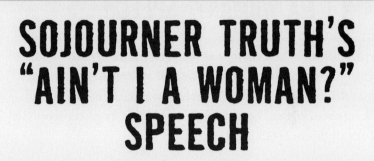

# SOJOURNER TRUTH'S "AIN'T I A WOMAN?" SPEECH

## MAY 1851

In 50 Words or Less! Delivered in 1851 by Sojourner Truth, an American woman born into slavery, this speech is memorable for its description of the hardships Truth endured as a slave. It's also important because Truth demands that she be treated like a woman and that women be treated as equals by men.

# SOJOURNER TRUTH'S "AIN'T I A WOMAN?" SPEECH

Well, children, where there is so much racket there must be something out of kilter **(out of line *or* out of order)**. I think that 'twixt the negroes of the South and the women at the North, all talking about rights, the white men will be in a fix pretty soon. But what's all this here talking about?

That man over there says that women need to be helped into carriages, and lifted over ditches, and to have the best place everywhere. Nobody ever helps me into carriages, or over mud-puddles, or gives me any best place! And ain't I a woman? Look at me! Look at my arm! I have ploughed and planted, and gathered into barns, and no man could head **(do better than)** me! And ain't I a woman? I could work as much and eat as much as a man—when I could get it—and bear the lash as well! And ain't I a woman? I have borne thirteen children, and seen most all sold off to slavery, and when I cried out with my mother's grief, none but Jesus heard me! And ain't I a woman?

Then they talk about this thing in the head; what's this they call it? [Member of audience whispers, "intellect."] That's it, honey. What's that got to do with women's rights or negroes' rights? If my cup won't hold but a pint, and yours holds a quart, wouldn't you be mean not to let me have my little half measure full?

**SUMMARY:** In the 1850s, it seemed pretty much everybody in America was unhappy. African Americans were unhappy because they were either slaves or they were free but concerned about their rights and the rights of their brothers and sisters still being held against their will. At the same time, women were unhappy because, despite what the Declaration of Independence said, they didn't enjoy the same rights as men. Many white men were unhappy because everybody was complaining to them about freeing the slaves and/or giving women the right to vote. And the white men who weren't unhappy about this complaining were unhappy because they sympathized with the complainers. They agreed with the minorities who weren't able to enjoy the full benefits of freedom.

Needless to say, there was a lot of unhappiness in the years leading up to the Civil War. Abolitionists were fighting to free the slaves while feminists were fighting for equality for women. Sojourner Truth is famous because she represented both. As a woman and a former slave, she was the perfect person to speak at the Women's Convention in Akron, Ohio. The convention was held in 1851 and is the sight of Truth's famous "Ain't I a Woman?" speech. (It should be noted that the document

Then that little man in black there, he says women can't have as much rights as men, 'cause Christ wasn't a woman! Where did your Christ come from? Where did your Christ come from? From God and a woman! Man had nothing to do with Him.

If the first woman God ever made was strong enough to turn the world upside down all alone, these women together ought to be able to turn it back, and get it right side up again! And now they is asking to do it, the men better let them.

Obliged **(Grateful)** to you for hearing me, and now old Sojourner ain't got nothing more to say. ★

here is based on recollections, or memories, of the speech, as no written draft exists.) This is an important historical text because it demonstrates just how strong the feelings of a mistreated person could be, especially when that mistreatment was completely legal under the laws of the U.S. government. Truth's brilliance as a public speaker is on display here as she decided to present her case not in a strong statement, as most people would choose to do, but with a question that has just one answer: yes. Yes, she is a woman.

Truth gave white men a warning—the kind of warning that made those who didn't believe in equal rights unhappy—when she said that they'd better beware "the negroes of the South and the women at the North." She was saying that these white men had been able to take advantage of slaves and women for a long time, but that time was coming to an end. There's just something beautifully American about this black woman having the guts to give white men the business like that. Back then, this sort of thing never happened! And of course, the crowd ate it up. They loved the speech, and they loved the question with the obvious answer ("And ain't I a woman?"), and they loved Sojourner Truth. How could they not? She talked about doing work in the fields—work that any man would be hard-pressed to do, and she tugged at the heartstrings, referring to the inner strength that helped her survive after watching most of her 13 children sold off to other slave owners.

Not only was Truth representative of the rebellious spirit of America, she displayed the character trait that Americans hold above all others: the ability to endure. People seem to appreciate a clever sense of humor, too, and Truth had one. Toward the end of her speech, she poked fun at "intellect"—even pretending to not know what the word meant—indicating to the crowd that brains had less to do with her argument than good ol' common sense. She used the example of the person with the quart sharing with her when she only had a pint which was her way of saying that with all that America has to offer, there should be plenty for everyone to share, women included.

Sojourner Truth gave our history books a text to look to when trying to understand what the nation was like before the Civil War, before the 13th Amendment settled the issue of slavery, and before the 19th Amendment gave women the right to vote. A lot of people are unhappy and a lot of people complain, but very few do it as powerfully and convincingly as Sojourner Truth. ★

**In Addition** . . . Sojourner Truth passed away in 1883, but in the years between the end of slavery and her death, she continued to stay politically active. Her main cause was trying to obtain land in the west for freed slaves. This grew out of the broken promise of "forty acres and a mule," made by a Union general, William T. Sherman, in response to their need for homes and work.

# What Others Have Said

In 1881, Frances Gage published her account of the "Ain't I a Woman?" speech in a book, *The History of Woman Suffrage*, which she co-wrote with famous feminist Susan B. Anthony. Her description of Sojourner Truth, upon completing the speech, reads:

> "Amid roars of applause, she returned to her corner, leaving more than one of us with streaming eyes, and hearts beating with gratitude. She had taken us up in her strong arms and carried us safely over the slough of difficulty turning the whole tide in our favor."

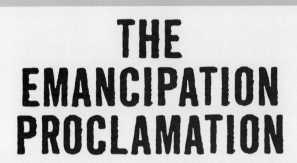

# THE EMANCIPATION PROCLAMATION

**JANUARY 1863**

**In 50 Words or Less!** The Emancipation Proclamation was not a law of Congress, but a declaration from President Abraham Lincoln. Announced during the second year of the Civil War, it freed all of the slaves in those states that had joined the Confederacy and contributed greatly to the eventual reunion of North and South.

# THE EMANCIPATION PROCLAMATION

By the President of the United States of America:

A Proclamation **(declaration)**.

Whereas, on the twenty-second day of September, in the year of our Lord one thousand eight hundred and sixty-two, a proclamation was issued by the President of the United States, containing, among other things, the following, to wit:

"That on the first day of January, in the year of our Lord one thousand eight hundred and sixty-three, **all persons held as slaves within any State or designated part of a State, the people whereof shall then be in rebellion against the United States, shall be then, thenceforward, and forever free;** and the Executive Government of the United States, including the military and naval authority thereof, will recognize and maintain the freedom of such persons, and will do no act or acts to repress **(limit)** such persons, or any of them, in any efforts they may make for their actual freedom."

"That the Executive will, on the first day of January aforesaid, by proclamation, designate the States and parts of States, if any, in which the people thereof, respectively, shall then be in rebellion against the United States; and the fact that any State, or the people thereof,

**SUMMARY:** Abraham Lincoln was inaugurated in January of 1861, the Confederate States of America named Jefferson Davis their president a month later, and in April, the first battle of the Civil War was fought at South Carolina's Fort Sumter. A few days later, Virginia became the first state to secede, or break away, from the Union.

While all of this was taking place, President Lincoln was being pressured by abolitionists (antislavery protesters) to free the slaves. Every once in a while, you'll find yourself in a situation that might seem easy to solve but actually involves complications that require great thought, complications that others might not see or understand. Though Lincoln would have liked to free the slaves immediately, he couldn't help but let politics come into play. And Honest Abe Lincoln was, at heart, a politician. But he was a politician on a noble mission.

Priority number one was to bring the country back together again. Lincoln couldn't just go ahead and free the slaves because if he did, that might mean more states seceding to join the Confederacy. If the Union was to win the war, Lincoln knew he had to hold on to as many states as possible.

shall on that day be, in good faith, represented in the Congress of the United States by members chosen thereto at elections wherein a majority of the qualified voters of such State shall have participated, shall, in the absence of strong countervailing **(opposing)** testimony, be deemed conclusive evidence that such State, and the people thereof, are not then in rebellion against the United States."

Now, therefore I, Abraham Lincoln, President of the United States, **by virtue of the power in me vested as Commander-in-Chief, of the Army and Navy of the United States in time of actual armed rebellion against the authority and government of the United States, and as a fit and necessary war measure for suppressing (smothering) said rebellion,** do, on this first day of January, in the year of our Lord one thousand eight hundred and sixty-three, and in accordance with my purpose so to do publicly proclaimed for the full period of one hundred days, from the day first above mentioned, order and designate as the States and parts of States wherein the people thereof respectively, are this day in rebellion against the United States, the following, to wit:

Arkansas, Texas, Louisiana, (**except** the Parishes **(counties)** of St. Bernard, Plaquemines, Jefferson, St. John, St. Charles, St. James, Ascension, Assumption, Terrebonne, Lafourche, St. Mary, St. Martin, and Orleans, including the City of New Orleans) Mississippi, Alabama, Florida, Georgia, South Carolina, North Carolina, and Virginia, (except the forty-eight counties designated as West Virginia,

He did want to free the slaves, though. And early in 1862, he shared his plan for emancipation with several of his cabinet members, including his trusted secretary of state, William H. Seward. By the fall of 1862, they were ready to go public, and on September 22, President Lincoln did just that, issuing his Emancipation Proclamation. This version was merely a verbal warning, though. (The part of the historical text that's in quotes is his declaration from that day.) It gave the slave states that had already seceded a "full period of one hundred days" notice that by January of 1863 all of their slaves would be granted their freedom. The first thing that Lincoln did in 1863 was put this proclamation on paper for the whole world to see, and on January 3 the slaves were officially emancipated. This earned Lincoln yet another nickname: The Great Emancipator.

The Emancipation Proclamation is, as its name suggests, a presidential proclamation and not an actual law. This is because it was never voted on and passed by Congress. Under the powers granted him during a time of war, it was legal for President Lincoln to free the slaves. He just had to wait for the right time to do so and could only enact this in certain parts of the country. For example, only those slaves being held in the states that were rebelling were now free. Lincoln even included a list of parishes, counties, and the city of New Orleans where the slaves would *not* be set free—at least not at that time. His exact words were, "for the present left precisely

and also the counties of Berkley, Accomac, Northampton, Elizabeth City, York, Princess Ann, and Norfolk, including the cities of Norfolk and Portsmouth), and which **excepted parts, are for the present, left precisely as if this proclamation were not issued.**

And by virtue of the power, and for the purpose aforesaid, I do order and declare that all persons held as slaves within said designated States, and parts of States, are, and henceforward shall be, free; and that **the Executive government of the United States, including the military and naval authorities thereof, will recognize and maintain the freedom of said persons.**

And I hereby enjoin **(command)** upon the people so declared to be free to abstain from all violence, unless in necessary self-defence; and I recommend to them that, in all cases when allowed, **they labor faithfully for reasonable wages.**

**And I further declare and make known, that such persons of suitable condition, will be received into the armed service of the United States to garrison forts, positions, stations, and other places, and to man vessels of all sorts in said service.**

And upon this act, sincerely believed to be an act of justice, warranted by the Constitution, upon military necessity, I invoke the considerate judgment of mankind, and the gracious favor of Almighty God.

as if this proclamation were not issued." The word *left* refers to the slaves being left alone, as still being property of their owners. Slave states that had not seceded from the Union were also allowed to keep their slaves. This was Lincoln's political effort to keep these states loyal to the Union.

Some states had put an end to slavery all on their own, but there were still thousands of slaves who had to wait until 1865, when the 13th Amendment was passed, before being granted their freedom. In 1863, though, the government's focus was on those slaves being held captive in the secessionist states. Not only were they freed, they now had the protection of the U.S. military which gave them a great sense of security. Many had been afraid to flee—until now. (Who could blame them for being scared and suspicious?)

The U.S. military stood to benefit from the Emancipation Proclamation in two ways. First, many of these slaves had been working, against their will, to support the Confederate Army with their farming, nursing, and factory work, and that source of labor was gone. Second, it now was legal for these men—for all African American men, in fact—to join the Union military. By war's end, 200,000 black men had joined up, contributing in whatever way they could to the defeat of the Confederacy. Another benefit of the Emancipation Proclamation, for the North, was that by freeing the slaves it

In witness whereof, I have hereunto set my hand and caused the seal of the United States to be affixed.

Done at the City of Washington, this first day of January, in the year of our Lord one thousand eight hundred and sixty three, and of the Independence of the United States of America the eighty-seventh. ★

was now impossible for the British and French to recognize the Confederate States of America as a legitimate country. They had both banned slavery already, and there was no way that Britain and France could justify being allies with a slave-friendly government. The British supplies stopped flowing to Confederate shores while the factories of the North continued to produce for the Union army. Lincoln's war machine chugged on while Jefferson Davis's began to sputter and cough.

There was one part of the Emancipation Proclamation that spoke directly to the freed slaves, and, in this paragraph, Lincoln almost sounds like a parent giving strongly worded advice. He suggested that they avoid violence at all costs and that they get to work ASAP! Lincoln knew that the Union could not support a large group of homeless and unemployed people. Even if the government was guilty of allowing slavery to exist in the past, there *was* a war going on. Resources were limited. So, Lincoln directed the freed slaves to "labor faithfully for reasonable wages." Lincoln wanted to bring a greater state of equality to the nation, but his priority was winning the war. Before ever becoming president, he'd quoted Jesus Christ in warning that "a house divided against itself cannot stand," and there was nothing more important to him than reuniting the country.

So, by freeing the slaves, President Lincoln was able to cripple the states that had seceded and take a step toward ending slavery once and for all. Of course, emancipating the slaves was a great humanitarian gesture, but in a land that was supposed to be "the land of the free," it's a step that came about 100 years and 15 presidents too late. That being said, the Emancipation Proclamation instantly made America a better country where a greater number of its citizens were now free to occupy themselves with "Life, Liberty and the pursuit of Happiness." ★

---

In Addition . . . Early in 1865, Congress passed the 13th Amendment that made slavery illegal in every part of the United States. By December 6 of that year, the necessary two-thirds of states had ratified (agreed to) the amendment and one of the most violent, disgraceful eras in American history was finally over.

---

# What Others Have Said

In 1967, Dr. Martin Luther King, Jr., said, "As long as the mind is enslaved, the body can never be free. Psychological freedom, a firm sense of self-esteem, is the most powerful weapon against the long night of physical slavery. No Lincolnian emancipation proclamation or Johnsonian civil rights bill can totally bring this kind of freedom. The negro will only be free when he reaches down to the inner depths of his own being and signs with the pen and ink of assertive manhood his own emancipation proclamation."

# GETTYSBURG ADDRESS

## NOVEMBER 1863

**In 50 Words or Less!** In 1863, President Abraham Lincoln gave one of the greatest speeches in U.S. history. And one of the shortest! His Gettysburg Address, at the dedication of the military cemetery in Gettysburg, Pennsylvania, paid tribute to deceased Union soldiers while reminding Americans why winning the Civil War was so important.

# GETTYSBURG ADDRESS

Four score and seven years ago **(87 years ago)** our fathers brought forth on this continent, a new nation, conceived in Liberty, and dedicated to the proposition **(statement)** that **all men are created equal.**

Now we are engaged in a great civil war, testing whether that nation, or any nation so conceived and so dedicated, can long endure **(survive)**. We are met on a great battle-field of that war. We have come to dedicate a portion of that field, as a final resting **place for those who here gave their lives that that nation might live.** It is altogether fitting and proper that we should do this.

But, in a larger sense, we can not dedicate—we can not consecrate **(bless)**—we can not hallow—this ground. The brave men, living and dead, who struggled here, have consecrated it, far above our poor power to add or detract. The world will little note, nor long remember what we say here, but it can never forget what they did here. **It is for us the living, rather, to be dedicated here to the unfinished work which they who fought here have thus far so nobly advanced.** It is rather for us to be here dedicated to the great task remaining before us—that from these honored dead we take increased devotion to that cause for which they gave the last full measure of devotion—that we here highly resolve **(decide)** that

**SUMMARY:** When President Abraham Lincoln issued his Emancipation Proclamation in January of 1863, the Union's war efforts were provided a boost. By the fall, however, there were still Confederate troops as far north as Pennsylvania. It was there that the Battle of Gettysburg took place. Though the Union was victorious, many lives were lost, and on November 19, 1863, the dedication of a military cemetery was held there. Lincoln delivered his Gettysburg Address to a small crowd gathered at the site where 45,000 men had died and, needless to say, the mood was quite somber.

Lincoln began his speech not by describing the details of the battle or how many soldiers had died, but by noting how much time had passed since the United States became a country. If you've ever heard the phrase "four score and seven years ago" (one score equals 20 years, so four score equals 80 years), you know exactly how many years it had been since the 13 colonies became 13 states, but you might be wondering, Why didn't Lincoln just say, "Eighty-seven years ago"?

Well, the answer is as simple as this: "Four score and seven years ago" sounds poetic and was far more appropriate for this serious occasion. In addition, Lincoln used a trick you might also employ when trying to memorize facts for a these dead shall not have died in vain—that this nation, under God, shall have a new birth of freedom—and that government of the people, by the people, for the people, shall not perish **(die)** from the earth. ★

test: he rhymed. That's right, the first two words—*four* and *score*—rhyme. It's a real attention getter and quite memorable, and in a way President Lincoln *did* help generations of students to study for generations of tests, sure to contain a question about this famous opening line. The final reason really shows how wise Lincoln was. By referring to the year in which it was written, signed, and sent off to Great Britain, he was challenging the nation to live up to the words of the Declaration of Independence. The opening paragraph ends with "dedicated to the proposition that all men are created equal." 'Nuff said!

It's also interesting to note the humility that Lincoln displayed in the third part of his speech when he said that nobody would "long remember what we say here." Like Thomas Paine trying to get the reader to focus on the words rather than the author, Lincoln was trying to keep the focus on the battles ahead rather than his speech or even the battles of the past. Clearly, his priority was winning the war and bringing the North and South back together again as the United States. He underestimated, though, the importance of his words. He couldn't have guessed that you'd still be studying them today. His words have certainly been long remembered.

"Four score and seven years ago" may be a wordy way to begin the speech, but the rest of Lincoln's Gettysburg Address is actually very brief. Edward Everett spoke before Lincoln and his speech lasted for two hours! But Lincoln's speech was so short that it ended before many in the crowd knew it had even begun. The Gettysburg Address took no more than three minutes to deliver and consisted of as few words as you'll find in a typical song (265 words, to be exact). Unlike most songs, the words he chose carried tremendous weight, and they are still being read seven score and a few years later.

Gettysburg might be the "final resting place" for many Americans, but through the efforts of leaders such as Lincoln, and the Americans he challenged to honor the dead with their continued devotion, the dream of freedom, equality, and a united America lived on. To be less than loyal, less than dedicated, Lincoln warned, would mean that the 45,000 who gave their lives at Gettysburg had died in vain.

In his final sentence, Lincoln stated that by winning the Civil War, freedom would survive as would democracy, which is a "government of the people, by the people, for the people." Sixteen months later, Lincoln was dead, assassinated by a southern actor named John Wilkes Booth. But, Booth was too late. Lincoln might not have survived his bullet, but the country was saved with North and South once again united. So, at least one of Lincoln's hopes came true: The dead had been honored with victory. And Lincoln, like those Union soldiers who perished at Gettysburg, did not die in vain. ★

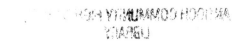

**In Addition** . . . Two copies of the Gettysburg Address are preserved in the Library of Congress and can be viewed, but not touched, by the public. A man named Dr. Nathan Stolow designed the two containers—made of stainless steel and Plexiglas—which use argon gas to keep the containers free of oxygen because oxidation ruins documents over time. The containers also filter out ultraviolet light, which can have a damaging effect. The temperature inside the containers is closely monitored, never rising above 50 degrees Fahrenheit, so as to guarantee that future generations will be able to see these original historical texts.

NOVEMBER 1863

# Who Would Write It Today?

Most people, even if they're not football fans, are familiar with the name Bill Belichick. This is because Belichick coached the New England Patriots to several Super Bowl championships. In 2003 and 2004, his team won 21 straight games, which is an NFL record. He was able to accomplish these things because he has a brilliant tactical mind—making tactical decisions in football is often compared to making tactical military decisions—and because he gives his team very inspirational speeches. He's able to convince his players that they can overcome great odds. In this regard, he is very similar to Abraham Lincoln. So, if someone were to write today's version of the Gettysburg Address, it would probably be Bill Belichick.

EXCERPT FROM MARK TWAIN'S

# THE ADVENTURES OF HUCKLEBERRY FINN

## 1884

**In 50 Words or Less!** In America's most famous coming-of-age story, Huck struggles with a moral dilemma: to treat Jim (a runaway slave) like property or a person. Because he's been such a good friend, Huck decides he'll risk being sent to hell, and rather than turning Jim in, Huck sets off to rescue him.

# EXCERPT FROM MARK TWAIN'S
# *THE ADVENTURES OF HUCKLEBERRY FINN*

WE dasn't stop again at any town for days and days; kept right along
down the river. We was down south in the warm weather now, and a
mighty long ways from home. We begun to come to trees with Span-
ish moss on them, hanging down from the limbs like long, gray beards.
It was the first I ever see it growing, and it made the woods look
solemn **(serious)** and dismal. So now the frauds **(fakers)** reckoned
they was out of danger, and they begun to work the villages again.

First they done a lecture on temperance **(self-control)**; but they
didn't make enough for them both to get drunk on. Then in another
village they started a dancing-school; but they didn't know no more
how to dance than a kangaroo does; so the first prance they made the
general public jumped in and pranced them out of town. Another
time they tried to go at yellocution **(public speaking)**; but they
didn't yellocute long till the audience got up and give them a solid
good cussing, and made them skip out. They tackled missionarying
**(preaching)**, and mesmerizing, and doctoring, and telling fortunes,
and a little of everything; but they couldn't seem to have no luck. So
at last they got just about dead broke, and laid around the raft as she
floated along, thinking and thinking, and never saying nothing, by the
half a day at a time, and dreadful blue and desperate.

**SUMMARY:** First, a little background: In this sequel to *The Adventures of Tom Sawyer,* Huckleberry Finn is living with his aunt because his father is not fit, according to the courts, to care for him. This is because he's a criminal and an alcoholic. In keeping with his character, Huck's father kidnaps him when he learns about the money Huck has now (he got it at the end of *Tom Sawyer*). After faking his death to escape from his father, Huck sets off on a raft for an adventure down the Mississippi River. Shortly into his journey, he runs into his aunt's slave, Jim, who decides to go with him. This makes Jim a runaway slave and Huck an accomplice to the crime. Several adventures await the pair, but also some degree of trouble.

The major plot point involves the King and the Duke, two small-time crooks who sell Jim for $40 of reward money. In this chapter, titled "You Can't Pray a Lie," Huck has to decide what's best: alerting his aunt so that Jim can be reclaimed or trying to rescue him himself, so that Jim doesn't get punished as a runaway slave and Huck treated like an outcast for aiding a runaway slave.

1884

And at last they took a change and begun to lay their heads together in the wigwam (tent) and talk low and confidential two or three hours at a time. Jim and me got uneasy. We didn't like the look of it. We judged they was studying up some kind of worse deviltry than ever. **We turned it over and over, and at last we made up our minds they was going to break into somebody's house or store, or was going into the counterfeit-money business, or something. So then we was pretty scared, and made up an agreement that we wouldn't have nothing in the world to do with such actions, and if we ever got the least show we would give them the cold shake and clear out and leave them behind.** Well, early one morning we hid the raft in a good, safe place about two mile below a little bit of a shabby village named Pikesville, and the king he went ashore and told us all to stay hid whilst he went up to town and smelt around to see if anybody had got any wind of the Royal Nonesuch there yet. ("House to rob, you MEAN," says I to myself; "and when you get through robbing it you'll come back here and wonder what has become of me and Jim and the raft—and you'll have to take it out in wondering.") And he said if he warn't back by midday the duke and me would know it was all right, and we was to come along.

So we stayed where we was. The duke he fretted and sweated around, and was in a mighty sour way. He scolded us for everything, and we couldn't seem to do nothing right; he found fault with every little thing. Something was a-brewing, sure. I was good and glad when midday come and no king; we could have a change, anyway—and maybe

It's in this chapter—Chapter 31—that *The Adventures of Huckleberry Finn* really establishes itself as a great American novel and certainly the country's finest coming-of-age story. The reason Chapter 31 is included in this book is because Huck's decision to put Jim's needs before his own is similar to America finally putting an end to legalized slavery. At the time that Twain wrote this book, America claimed that "all men are created equal," but it certainly wasn't a place that treated all men equally. ("And what about the women?" Sojourner Truth would ask!) Huck doesn't make any great statements against slavery or racism, but he does take a step in the right direction. America had done the same, with its victory in the Civil War and with passing of the 13th, 14th, and 15th Amendments, but still had a ways to go.

Twain is particularly funny when using the dialect (or spoken language) of the time. Unfortunately, this includes using the word *nigger,* but it's important to the story that the dialogue sound legitimate. There are other aspects of the book that you might find kind of confusing, given your experiences in modern day America. For example, earlier in the book, Huck feels bad about making his aunt worry about her slave. He says nothing about feeling bad about Jim having to *be* a slave, but Huck can't really be blamed for feeling this way, given how young he is and the fact that he was raised in a world where people owned other people as property.

1884

a chance for THE chance on top of it. So me and the duke went up to the village, and hunted around there for the king, and by and by we found him in the back room of a little low doggery, very tight, and a lot of loafers bullyragging him for sport, and he a-cussing and a-threatening with all his might, and so tight he couldn't walk, and couldn't do nothing to them. The duke he begun to abuse him for an old fool, and the king begun to sass **(talk)** back, and the minute they was fairly at it I lit out and shook the reefs out of my hind legs, and spun down the river road like a deer, for I see our chance; and I made up my mind that it would be a long day before they ever see me and Jim again. I got down there all out of breath but loaded up with joy, and sung out:

"Set her loose, Jim! we're all right now!"

But there warn't no answer, and nobody come out of the wigwam. Jim was gone! I set up a shout—and then another—and then another one; and run this way and that in the woods, whooping and screeching; but it warn't no use—old Jim was gone. Then I set down and cried; I couldn't help it. But I couldn't set still long. Pretty soon I went out on the road, trying to think what I better do, and I run across a boy walking, and asked him if he'd seen a strange nigger dressed so and so, and he says:

"Yes."

"Whereabouts?" says I.

What is moral and what is not is established by society, and in feeling bad about helping to free another human being from slavery, Huck is reflecting the values of that time and place. Twain is extremely convincing in this chapter, writing a monologue in which Huck struggles with acting "morally" (i.e., telling his aunt where Jim is so she can reclaim him) or acting "immorally" (i.e., continuing to break the law by helping Jim).

Part of the concern Huck has about returning Jim to his aunt as a runaway slave is that "everybody naturally despises an ungrateful nigger." He says "ungrateful" because people who owned slaves thought that the slaves had a pretty good life. To make matters even more confusing, Huck also has some concerns for himself. He cares about Jim, but if people at home found out he'd helped a runaway slave they would harass him for the rest of his life. Twain is being brutally honest about the thoughts running through Huck's head and because he was honest about things such as Huck's self-concern and the moral teachings of the time, Huckleberry Finn is one of the most memorable characters in American literature. If the book wasn't that good, you wouldn't be reading about it here!

The name of the chapter comes from the monologue in which Huck asks God for guidance, only to come to the realization that "you can't pray a lie." In trying to figure out why he can't come up with the right words to pray, he says: "I knowed very

1884

**"Down to Silas Phelps' place, two mile below here. He's a runaway nigger, and they've got him. Was you looking for him?"**

"You bet I ain't! I run across him in the woods about an hour or two ago, and he said if I hollered he'd cut my livers out—and told me to lay down and stay where I was; and I done it. Been there ever since; afeard to come out."

"Well," he says, "you needn't be afeard no more, becuz they've got him. He run off f'm down South, som'ers."

"It's a good job they got him."

"Well, I RECKON! There's two hunderd dollars reward on him. It's like picking up money out'n the road."

"Yes, it is—and I could a had it if I'd been big enough; I see him FIRST. Who nailed him?"

"It was an old fellow—a stranger—and he sold out his chance in him for forty dollars, becuz he's got to go up the river and can't wait. Think o' that, now! You bet I'D wait, if it was seven year."

"That's me, every time," says I. "But maybe his chance ain't worth no more than that, if he'll sell it so cheap. Maybe there's something ain't straight **(legitimate)** about it."

well why they wouldn't come. It was because my heart warn't right; it was because I warn't square; it was because I was playing double." He decides that God knows what's really in his heart and in his mind, so there's no point in trying to fib his way around it. The words won't come because he's a bad person. He talks about "being brung up wicked" and about how he could've gone to Sunday school like his aunt wanted him to, but didn't. Huck has acted immorally in the past and he figures he might as well act immorally now. The difference between his wrong doing of before and now is that this time, he's actually acting in a way that the reader knows is moral.

It's a classic turn of events when Huck rips up the letter telling his aunt where Jim is so that she can reclaim him. According to everything he's been taught, by ripping up that letter and helping out another human being, he's damning himself to hell! But if that's the way it's gonna be, that's the way it's gonna be, he decides. Huck's plan is to "steal Jim out of slavery" and then they'll return home and just make some excuse about where they've been. This way, Jim won't be treated as a runaway slave and Huck won't be considered an accomplice. The build-up to Huck's big coming-of-age decision is a confession about his feelings for Jim: "But somehow I couldn't seem to strike no places to harden me against him, but only the other kind." The "other kind" would be the soft places—the memories of all the things he and Jim have been through together.

"But it IS, though—straight as a string. I see the handbill myself. It tells all about him, to a dot—paints him like a picture, and tells the plantation he's frum, below NewrLEANS **(New Orleans)**. No-sir-ree-BOB, they ain't no trouble 'bout THAT speculation, you bet you. Say, gimme a chaw tobacker, won't ye?"

I didn't have none, so he left. I went to the raft, and set down in the wigwam to think. But I couldn't come to nothing. I thought till I wore my head sore, but I couldn't see no way out of the trouble. After all this long journey, and after all we'd done for them scoundrels, here it was all come to nothing, everything all busted up and ruined, because they could have the heart to serve Jim such a trick as that, and make him a slave again all his life, and amongst strangers, too, for forty dirty dollars.

Once I said to myself it would be a thousand times better for Jim to be a slave at home where his family was, as long as he'd GOT to be a slave, and so I'd better write a letter to Tom Sawyer and tell him to tell Miss Watson where he was. But I soon give up that notion for two things: she'd be mad and disgusted at his rascality **(mischief)** and ungratefulness for leaving her, and so she'd sell him straight down the river again; and if she didn't, **everybody naturally despises an ungrateful nigger, and they'd make Jim feel it all the time, and so he'd feel ornery (grouchy) and disgraced. And then think of ME! It would get all around that Huck Finn helped a nigger to get his freedom; and if I was ever to see anybody from that town again I'd be ready to get down and lick his boots for shame.** That's just the

He thinks about how happy he made Jim when he helped him and how Jim said he was his best friend. A guy like Huck has to say the "other kind" rather than "soft places." He's a tough kid, but he's got a big heart. You probably know someone like him, someone who gets into trouble with the teachers but whose friends can count on him or her. Huck's heart is so big, in fact, that he even feels bad when he sees King and Duke get tarred and feathered. These are criminals that held Huck and Jim against their will, that stole from people mourning a dead relative, that go from town to town cheating folks out of their money, that sold Jim for $40 and didn't care at all that he'd end up back in slavery, yet Huck was upset by the cruelty he was witnessing. Slowly but surely he was growing up, becoming more sensitive toward others and even developing a sense of fairness and justice, just as America was. ★

1884

way: a person does a low-down thing, and then he don't want to take no consequences **(responsibility)** of it. Thinks as long as he can hide, it ain't no disgrace. That was my fix exactly. The more I studied about this the more my conscience went to grinding me, and the more wicked and low-down and ornery I got to feeling. And at last, when it hit me all of a sudden that here was the plain hand of Providence slapping me in the face and letting me know my wickedness was being watched all the time from up there in heaven, whilst I was stealing a poor old woman's nigger that hadn't ever done me no harm, and now was showing me there's One that's always on the lookout, and ain't a-going to allow no such miserable doings to go only just so fur and no further, I most dropped in my tracks I was so scared. Well, I tried the best I could to kinder soften it up somehow for myself by saying I was brung up wicked, and so I warn't so much to blame; but something inside of me kept saying, "There was the Sunday-school, you could a gone to it; and if you'd a done it they'd a learnt you there that people that acts as I'd been acting about that nigger goes to everlasting fire."

**It made me shiver. And I about made up my mind to pray, and see if I couldn't try to quit being the kind of a boy I was and be better. So I kneeled down. But the words wouldn't come. Why wouldn't they? It warn't no use to try and hide it from Him. Nor from ME, neither. I knowed very well why they wouldn't come. It was because my heart warn't right; it was because I warn't square; it was because I was playing double. I was letting ON to give up sin, but away inside of me I was holding on to the biggest one of all.**

**I was trying to make my mouth SAY I would do the right thing and the clean thing, and go and write to that nigger's owner and tell where he was; but deep down in me I knowed it was a lie, and He knowed it. You can't pray a lie—I found that out.**

So I was full of trouble, full as I could be; and didn't know what to do. At last I had an idea; and I says, I'll go and write the letter—and then see if I can pray. Why, it was astonishing, the way I felt as light as a feather right straight off, and my troubles all gone. So I got a piece of paper and a pencil, all glad and excited, and set down and wrote:

> *Miss Watson, your runaway nigger Jim is down here two mile below Pikesville, and Mr. Phelps has got him and he will give him up for the reward if you send.*
> *HUCK FINN.*

I felt good and all washed clean of sin for the first time I had ever felt so in my life, and I knowed I could pray now. But I didn't do it straight off, but laid the paper down and set there thinking—thinking how good it was all this happened so, and how near I come to being lost and going to hell. And went on thinking. And got to thinking over our trip down the river; and I see Jim before me all the time: in the day and in the night-time, sometimes moonlight, sometimes storms, and we a-floating along, talking and singing and laughing. But somehow I couldn't seem to strike no places to harden me against him, but only the other kind. I'd see him standing my watch on top of his'n, 'stead of calling me, so I could go on sleeping; and see him how glad he was when I come back out of the fog; and when I come to him again in the swamp, up there where the feud was; and such-like times; and would always call me honey, and pet me and do everything he could think of for me, and how good he always was; and at last I struck the time I saved him by telling the men we had small-pox aboard, and **he was so grateful, and said I was the best friend old Jim ever had in the world, and the ONLY one he's got now;** and then I happened to look around and see that paper.

It was a close place. I took it up, and held it in my hand. I was a-trembling, because I'd got to decide, forever, betwixt two things, and I knowed it. I studied a minute, sort of holding my breath, and then says to myself:

**"All right, then, I'll GO to hell"**—and tore it up.

It was awful thoughts and awful words, but they was said. And I let them stay said; and never thought no more about reforming. I shoved the whole thing out of my head, and said I would take up wickedness again, which was in my line, being brung up to it, and the other warn't. **And for a starter I would go to work and steal Jim out of slavery again; and if I could think up anything worse, I would do that, too; because as long as I was in, and in for good, I might as well go the whole hog.** ★

In Addition . . . The book ends with Huck dreaming of more adventures with Tom and Jim. It also features Twain's last dig at America's idea of being civilized: "But I reckon I got to light out for the Territory ahead of the rest, because Aunt Sally she's going to adopt me and sivilize me, and I can't stand it. I been there before."

1884

# What Others Have Said

One of the reasons *The Adventures of Huckleberry Finn* is still widely read in schools is that there are aspects of the book that can be debated, including whether or not Twain was a racist. His critics say that Jim talked and acted like all of the typical racial stereotypes. Twain's supporters say he was just writing about the society he lived in. One of these supporters, book reviewer Shelley Fisher Fishkin, states, "The power of *Huckleberry Finn* to engage Americans in debates about freedom and race so many years after it was written testifies to this fact."

# UPTON SINCLAIR'S THE JUNGLE

## 1906

**In 50 Words or Less!** In Chapter 2 of Sinclair's revealing novel, Jurgis Rudkus is introduced to the awful sights, sounds, and smells of Chicago's stockyards and boarding houses. Despite the filth and overcrowding, he's optimistic about making his American dream come true. In later chapters, though, that dream crumbles into reality.

# EXCERPT FROM UPTON SINCLAIR'S *THE JUNGLE*

A full hour before the party reached the city they had begun to note the perplexing **(confusing)** changes in the atmosphere. It grew darker all the time, and upon the earth the grass seemed to grow less green. Every minute, as the train sped on, the colors of things became dingier; the fields were grown parched and yellow, **the landscape hideous and bare. And along with the thickening smoke they began to notice another circumstance, a strange, pungent odor.** They were not sure that it was unpleasant, this odor; some might have called it sickening, but their taste in odors was not developed, and they were only sure that it was curious. Now, sitting in the trolley car, they realized that they were on their way to the home of it—that they had traveled all the way from Lithuania to it. It was now no longer something far off and faint, that you caught in whiffs; you could literally taste it, as well as smell it—you could take hold of it, almost, and examine it at your leisure. They were divided in their opinions about it. It was an elemental **(basic)** odor, raw and crude; it was rich, almost rancid, sensual, and strong. There were some who drank it in as if it were an intoxicant; there were others who put their handkerchiefs to their faces. The new emigrants were still tasting it, lost in wonder, when suddenly the car came to a halt, and the door was flung open, and a voice shouted—"Stockyards!"

**SUMMARY:** Before Upton Sinclair's *The Jungle,* the terms *prime* and *Grade A* weren't associated with beef. Although he wanted his work to be an eye opener about the working conditions of the poor, Sinclair's book actually had a greater impact on the food produced by, and the conditions within, America's meat packing plants. As they read, people realized they were paying for food that could actually harm them. Plus, it was gross! Now, we know to only buy meat that's marked prime or Grade A, but you would've been wise, in the days before *The Jungle,* to avoid hot dogs, hamburgers, and sausage. Unless, of course, you liked to eat rat tails.

Muckraking is journalism that digs up the dirt, exposing the filth of scandals and indecent behavior. And in *The Jungle,* there's plenty of dirt and filth. Sinclair's book might be fiction, but it was based on fact and is thus considered one of the greatest pieces of social journalism ever written. It's memorable muckraking for two reasons. One, *The Jungle* exposed the awful conditions of America's meat packing plants. Two, it described how hard it was for immigrants to make the American dream come true. In this chapter, Jurgis Rudkus brings his wife and her family to the New World and their trip is filled with talk of a

**1906**

They were left standing upon the corner, staring; down a side street there were two rows of brick houses, and between them a vista: half a dozen chimneys, tall as the tallest of buildings, touching the very sky—and leaping from them half a dozen columns of smoke, thick, oily, and black as night. It might have come from the center of the world, this smoke, where the fires of the ages still smolder. It came as if self-impelled, driving all before it, a perpetual **(continuous)** explosion. It was inexhaustible; one stared, waiting to see it stop, but still the great streams rolled out. They spread in vast clouds overhead, writhing, curling; then, uniting in one giant river, they streamed away down the sky, stretching a black pall **(cloud)** as far as the eye could reach.

Then the party became aware of another strange thing. This, too, like the color, was a thing elemental; it was a sound, a sound made up of ten thousand little sounds. You scarcely noticed it at first—it sunk into your consciousness, a vague disturbance, a trouble. It was like the murmuring of the bees in the spring, the whisperings of the forest; it suggested endless activity, the rumblings of a world in motion. It was only by an effort that one could realize that it was made by animals, that it was the distant lowing of ten thousand cattle, the distant grunting of ten thousand swine **(pigs)**.

They would have liked to follow it up, but, alas, they had no time for adventures just then. **The policeman on the corner was beginning to watch them; and so, as usual, they started up the street.** Scarcely

fellow Lithuanian who has already made his dream come true. By the end of the chapter, there's still great hope, although their dream quickly turns into a nightmare.

The second chapter was chosen as a historical text because it describes industrial America and, in particular, the working and living conditions of the employees of meat packing plants. When the Rudkus family arrives in Packingtown, they see smoke billowing out of smoke stacks above and the masses of people trying to survive on the filthy ground below. A train carries them to the outskirts of Chicago, at the same time carrying the reader back to an era when health conditions weren't as strictly regulated as they are today. It might be hard for you to imagine living as these people did, but it's really the way things were. Just as there was once slavery in America, children *did* play in trash heaps. This isn't something any foreigner ever expected when deciding to move to the New World, and there can be no doubt that the dreams the Rudkus family had in mind were no different than those of any other immigrant. The disappointments they experienced were no different, either.

When he arrived with his family, Jurgis Rudkus quickly realized that the high wages he might earn were accompanied by high prices. He also didn't think ahead and was shocked to learn that the money he'd saved in his home country of Lithuania

had they gone a block, however, before Jonas was heard to give a cry, and began pointing excitedly across the street. Before they could gather the meaning of his breathless ejaculations he had bounded away, and they saw him enter a shop, over which was a sign: "J. Szedvilas, Delicatessen." When he came out again it was in company with a very stout gentleman in shirt sleeves and an apron, clasping Jonas by both hands and laughing hilariously. Then Teta Elzbieta recollected suddenly that Szedvilas had been the name of the mythical friend who had made his fortune in America. To find that he had been making it in the delicatessen business was an extraordinary piece of good fortune at this juncture; though it was well on in the morning, they had not breakfasted, and the children were beginning to whimper.

Thus was the happy ending to a woeful **(unhappy)** voyage. The two families literally fell upon each other's necks—for it had been years since Jokubas Szedvilas had met a man from his part of Lithuania. Before half the day they were lifelong friends. Jokubas understood all the pitfalls of this new world, and could explain all of its mysteries; he could tell them the things they ought to have done in the different emergencies—and what was still more to the point, he could tell them what to do now. He would take them to poni Aniele, who kept a boardinghouse the other side of the yards; **old Mrs. Jukniene, he explained, had not what one would call choice accommodations, but they might do for the moment. To this Teta Elzbieta hastened to respond that nothing could be too cheap to suit them just then; for they were quite terrified over the sums they had had to**

would not buy much in his new, more expensive country. Sinclair describes the realization, and the disappointment, as such: " . . . and so were really being cheated by the world!" Many of today's immigrants have learned their lesson well, earning American dollars and sending them back home where they have far greater value.

There are parts of the book that you might be able to relate to, even if you aren't an immigrant. For example, "The policeman on the corner was beginning to watch them; and so, as usual, they started up the street." With this simple sentence, Sinclair captures one of the many stresses experienced by new immigrants, and it's a way you might have felt some time when you were hanging out and a police officer walked by. Like the Rudkus family, you and your friends probably decided it was better to move on than risk getting in trouble.

The successful Lithuanian (who owns a deli in Packingtown) led the family to a boarding house and on the way, they viewed the shocking living conditions of their new neighborhood while hearing about the shocking living conditions of the boarding house. As they walked, for example, they were overwhelmed by the smell of garbage and the flies it attracted, "literally blackening the air." Just as the air was crowded with flies, just as the streets were crowded with people, the rooms in the boarding houses were crowded. To make matters worse,

1906

**expend.** A very few days of practical experience in this land of high wages had been sufficient to make clear to them the cruel fact that it was also a land of high prices, and that in it the poor man was almost as poor as in any other corner of the earth; and so there vanished in a night all the wonderful dreams of wealth that had been haunting Jurgis. **What had made the discovery all the more painful was that they were spending, at American prices, money which they had earned at home rates of wages—and so were really being cheated by the world!** The last two days they had all but starved themselves—it made them quite sick to pay the prices that the railroad people asked them for food.

Yet, when they saw the home of the Widow Jukniene they could not but recoil **(wince)**, even so, in all their journey they had seen nothing so bad as this. Poni Aniele had a four-room flat in one of that wilderness of two-story frame tenements that lie "back of the yards." There were four such flats in each building, and each of the four was a "boardinghouse" for the occupancy of foreigners—Lithuanians, Poles, Slovaks, or Bohemians. Some of these places were kept by private persons, some were cooperative. There would be an average of half a dozen boarders to each room—sometimes there were thirteen or fourteen to one room, fifty or sixty to a flat. Each one of the occupants furnished his own accommodations—that is, a mattress and some bedding. The mattresses would be spread upon the floor in rows—and there would be nothing else in the place except a stove. **It was by no means unusual for two men to own the**

the mattresses themselves could get pretty crowded. Sinclair explains how one man might share his with another man: If one worked the night shift, he could take the mattress during the day while the other man worked and vice versa.

The boardinghouse was so dirty that there were jokes made about the landlady's method for cleaning: She kept chickens and would let them into the rooms to eat the bed bugs. This is an example of humor as a means of coping with an awful situation. Jokes might be told while hanging out on the street after work, but the people of Packingtown didn't just hang out on the streets to socialize. During the warm summer months, they slept there! This is because the only thing worse than mattresses covering the floor of a room is mattresses covering the floor of a room in 100-degree heat. So, residents went from the bed bugs to the flies. Essentially, there was no escape from the vermin.

As you can probably guess, the kids living in Packingtown had few options for fun. They could play in filthy puddles of mud and human waste, in a pond of run-off water (that is, grossly enough, sold as ice in the winter), or on the exposed part of the garbage dump that Packingtown is built on. Yes, they built this part of Chicago on a garbage dump. The kids there can be seen searching for food—observers aren't sure if it's food for themselves or animals at home—and they have plenty of

1906

**same mattress in common, one working by day and using it by night, and the other working at night and using it in the daytime.** Very frequently a lodging house keeper would rent the same beds to double shifts of men.

Mrs. Jukniene was a wizened-up little woman, with a wrinkled face. Her home was unthinkably filthy; you could not enter by the front door at all, owing to the mattresses, and when you tried to go up the backstairs you found that she had walled up most of the porch with old boards to make a place to keep her chickens. **It was a standing jest (joke) of the boarders that Aniele cleaned house by letting the chickens loose in the rooms. Undoubtedly this did keep down the vermin (pests), but it seemed probable, in view of all the circumstances, that the old lady regarded it rather as feeding the chickens than as cleaning the rooms.** The truth was that she had definitely given up the idea of cleaning anything, under pressure of an attack of rheumatism, which had kept her doubled up in one corner of her room for over a week; during which time eleven of her boarders, heavily in her debt, had concluded to try their chances of employment in Kansas City.

This was July, and the fields were green. One never saw the fields, nor any green thing whatever, in Packingtown; but one could go out on the road and "hobo it," as the men phrased it, and see the country, and have a long rest, and an easy time riding on the freight cars.

time for foraging because there's nobody around to make them go to school. As a matter of fact, Sinclair explains that there wasn't any place available for them to get an education, even if they wanted one: " . . . you thought there must be a school just out, and it was only after long acquaintance that you were able to realize that there was no school." And before you get too jealous, keep in mind that the only way for people to make a better life for themselves is through education. Without a school, there could be no hope of ending the cycle of poverty.

Going to school is, indeed, a part of the American dream, but nothing symbolizes this dream more than buying your own home. At one point, toward the beginning of the chapter, Rudkus says that he really wants to buy a house. And he's willing to work for it, too. Nobody in this book expected to be given a home. They weren't counting on winning the lottery or anything like that. But as the book continues, the Rudkus family learns that no amount of hard work will ever get them their riches. Even with Rudkus's wife prostituting herself, they won't ever be able to afford their own home.

Despite all of this, Sinclair's characters, like many real life immigrants, respect America's moneymaking society. The reader can see how disgusting it is that bricks are made from the contaminated soil and that ice is made from the filthy water, but the Rudkus family is impressed by all of this

Such was the home to which the new arrivals were welcomed. There was nothing better to be had—they might not do so well by looking further, for Mrs. Jukniene had at least kept one room for herself and her three little children, and now offered to share this with the women and the girls of the party. **They could get bedding at a secondhand store, she explained; and they would not need any, while the weather was so hot—doubtless they would all sleep on the sidewalk such nights as this, as did nearly all of her guests.**

"Tomorrow," Jurgis said, when they were left alone, "tomorrow I will get a job, and perhaps Jonas will get one also; and then we can get a place of our own."

Later that afternoon he and Ona went out to take a walk and look about them, to see more of this district which was to be their home. In back of the yards the dreary two-story frame houses were scattered farther apart, and there were great spaces bare—that seemingly had been overlooked by the great sore of a city as it spread itself over the surface of the prairie. These bare places were grown up with dingy, yellow weeds, hiding innumerable tomato cans; innumerable children played upon them, chasing one another here and there, screaming and fighting. **The most uncanny thing about this neighborhood was the number of the children; you thought there must be a school just out, and it was only after long acquaintance that you were able to realize that there was no school,** but that these were the children of the neighborhood—that there were so many children to the block

industriousness. It's only in later chapters that they realize the factory owners use them just as the ice and bricks are used; that they are nothing more than moneymaking tools and that they aren't the ones making the money.

Just as with Twain's fictional contribution to this history book, it goes without saying that sometimes people learn best from a story. There can be no doubt that Sinclair wanted the American people—including those in the government—to learn from his story. At the same time, the young writer never could've dreamed that his book would be so successful. Just like Jurgis Rudkus, Sinclair had his dreams; but unlike Rudkus,

**1906**

in Packingtown that nowhere on its streets could a horse and buggy move faster than a walk!

It could not move faster anyhow, on account of the state of the streets. Those through which Jurgis and Ona were walking resembled streets less than they did a miniature topographical **(elevation)** map. The roadway was commonly several feet lower than the level of the houses, which were sometimes joined by high board walks; there were no pavements—there were mountains and valleys and rivers, gullies and ditches, and great hollows full of stinking green water. In these pools the children played, and rolled about in the mud of the streets; here and there one noticed them digging in it, after trophies which they had stumbled on. **One wondered about this, as also about the swarms of flies which hung about the scene, literally blackening the air, and the strange, fetid odor which assailed one's nostrils, a ghastly odor, of all the dead things of the universe. It impelled the visitor to questions and then the residents would explain, quietly, that all this was "made" land, and that it had been "made" by using it as a dumping ground for the city garbage.** After a few years the unpleasant effect of this would pass away, it was said; but meantime, in hot weather—and especially when it rained—the flies were apt to be annoying. Was it not unhealthful? the stranger would ask, and the residents would answer, "Perhaps; but there is no telling."

Upton Sinclair's came true. He was even invited to the White House after President Theodore Roosevelt was swamped with letters calling for improvements in the meat packing industry. Upon the success of his self-published book, Sinclair made the comment, "I aimed at the public's heart, and by accident I hit it in the stomach." Indeed he did. ★

In Addition . . . *The Jungle* contributed to the passing of the Pure Food and Drugs Act and Meat Inspection Act in 1906. Now, there are eight grades of meat, as determined by the United States Department of Agriculture (USDA). Only the top three grades are familiar to the regular grocery store shopper; these are *select, choice,* and *prime,* with prime being the best. The grade is based on the quality of the meat, which wasn't ever determined before Sinclair's novel.

1906

A little way farther on, and Jurgis and Ona, staring open-eyed and wondering, came to the place where this "made" ground was in process of making. Here was a great hole, perhaps two city blocks square, and with long files of garbage wagons creeping into it. The place had an odor for which there are no polite words; and it was sprinkled over with children, who raked in it from dawn till dark. Sometimes visitors from the packing houses would wander out to see this "dump," and they would stand by and debate as to whether the children were eating the food they got, or merely collecting it for the chickens at home. Apparently none of them ever went down to find out.

Beyond this dump there stood a great brickyard, with smoking chimneys. First they took out the soil to make bricks, and then they filled it up again with garbage, which seemed to Jurgis and Ona a felicitous **(fortunate)** arrangement, characteristic of an enterprising country like America. A little way beyond was another great hole, which they had emptied and not yet filled up. This held water, and all summer it stood there, with the near-by soil draining into it, festering and stewing in the sun; and then, when winter came, somebody cut the ice on it, and sold it to the people of the city. **This, too, seemed to the newcomers an economical (efficient) arrangement; for they did not read the newspapers, and their heads were not full of troublesome thoughts about "germs."**

They stood there while the sun went down upon this scene, and the sky in the west turned blood-red, and the tops of the houses shone like fire.

Jurgis and Ona were not thinking of the sunset, however—their backs were turned to it, and all their thoughts were of Packingtown, which they could see so plainly in the distance. The line of the buildings stood clear-cut and black against the sky; here and there out of the mass rose the great chimneys, with the river of smoke streaming away to the end of the world. It was a study in colors now, this smoke; in the sunset light it was black and brown and gray and purple. All the sordid (disgusting) suggestions of the place were gone—in the twilight it was a vision of power. **To the two who stood watching while the darkness swallowed it up, it seemed a dream of wonder, with its talc of human energy, of things being done, of employment for thousands upon thousands of men, of opportunity and freedom, of life and love and joy. When they came away, arm in arm, Jurgis was saying, "Tomorrow I shall go there and get a job!"** ★

# What Others Have Said

George Orwell was heavily influenced by Upton Sinclair, and this is evident in his novel, *Animal Farm,* which shares many themes with *The Jungle.* More recently, Eric Schlosser's nonfiction book, *Fast Food Nation,* might also remind you of Sinclair's book because he describes the Central American immigrants who work in food processing and also the not-so-appetizing ingredients in the typical hamburger.

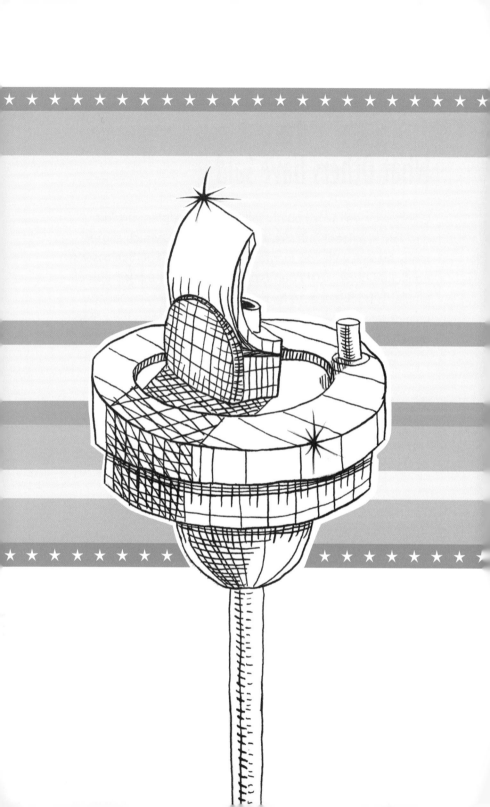

EXCERPT FROM

# BROWN V. BOARD OF EDUCATION

## MAY 1954

**In 50 Words or Less!** In 1954, the Supreme Court decided on this case after learning about the long-term damage that was being done to black children not allowed to attend the same schools as white children. The court said that segregation is unconstitutional, making this the first victory of the modern civil rights movement.

# EXCERPT FROM *BROWN V. BOARD OF EDUCATION*

Such considerations apply with added force to children in grade and high schools. **To separate them from others of similar age and qualifications solely because of their race generates a feeling of inferiority (weakness) as to their status in the community that may affect their hearts and minds in a way unlikely ever to be undone.** The effect of this separation on their educational opportunities was well stated by a finding in the Kansas case by a court which nevertheless felt compelled **(required)** to rule against the Negro plaintiffs:

"Segregation of white and colored children in public schools has a detrimental **(negative)** effect upon the colored children. The impact is greater when it has the sanction **(approval)** of the law; for the policy of separating the races is usually interpreted as denoting the inferiority of the negro group. A sense of inferiority affects the motivation of a child to learn. **Segregation with the sanction of law, therefore, has a tendency to [retard] the educational and mental development of negro children** and to deprive them of some of the benefits they would receive in a racial[ly] integrated school system."

Whatever may have been the extent of psychological knowledge at the time of *Plessy v. Ferguson,* this finding is amply **(thoroughly)**

**SUMMARY:** Before becoming a Supreme Court justice, Thurgood Marshall was an attorney for the National Association for the Advancement of Colored People (NAACP), and in 1954 he won his greatest case, helping black children to gain access to the same schools as white children. Our nation was truly changed by the *Brown v. Board of Education of Topeka Kansas* decision, and that's why, of the many important cases argued before the Supreme Court, *Brown v. Board of Education* is included in the book.

It's true that many people have been impacted by this case, but you might not know that many people were involved in smaller cases leading up to the one finally argued before the highest court in the land. A "class action" is when people file a complaint, in a court, for themselves and anybody else suffering from a similar problem—the suit against the tobacco companies is one example—and *Brown v. Board of Education* was a class action. This is because in order to be considered by the Supreme Court, cases from four different states and Washington, DC, had to be lumped together into one. Oliver Brown was a father from Topeka, and he wanted his daughter to be able to go to the same school as white children. Even

supported by modern authority. Any language in *Plessy v. Ferguson* contrary to this finding is rejected.

**We conclude that in the field of public education the doctrine of "separate but equal" has no place. Separate educational facilities are inherently unequal.** Therefore, we hold that the plaintiffs and others similarly situated for whom the actions have been brought are, by reason of the segregation complained of, deprived of the equal protection of the laws guaranteed by the Fourteenth Amendment. This disposition **(description)** makes unnecessary any discussion whether such segregation also violates the Due Process Clause of the Fourteenth Amendment.

Because these are class actions, because of the wide applicability of this decision, and because of the great variety of local conditions, the formulation of decrees in these cases presents problems of considerable complexity. On reargument, the consideration of appropriate relief was necessarily subordinated **(given less consideration)** to the primary question—the constitutionality of segregation in public education. **We have now announced that such segregation is a denial of the equal protection of the laws.** In order that we may have the full assistance of the parties in formulating decrees **(rulings)**, the cases will be restored to the docket, and the parties are requested to present further argument on Questions 4 and 5 previously propounded **(submitted)** by the Court for the reargument this Term. The Attorney General of the United States is again invited to within Kansas, there were 12 different segregation cases that the courts had heard over the past 50 years. With the NAACP on board, though, the cases started getting the attention they deserved on a national level. Brown was chosen as the lead plaintiff because he was a man and the NAACP thought that would help their case to be heard (the Supreme Court doesn't accept all cases), and they were right. Marshall described for Chief Justice Earl Warren and the other justices the conditions in the schools that black children attended; he described for them the ways in which black people still weren't receiving all of the rights granted to them by the 14th and 15th Amendments.

Though the Union had won the Civil War and the slaves were freed, and though the 15th Amendment gave black Americans the right to vote, our country was still a long way away from being a place where "all men are created equal." (Mark Twain would've been quite disappointed.) In many states, Jim Crow laws kept black people from voting and enforced legalized segregation. Even 40 years after the Civil War ended, the Supreme Court was making decisions like *Plessy v. Ferguson* (1896), which established the idea of "separate but equal." Basically, this meant that America thought that black children could be educated separately from white children yet receive an equal education. It meant that black people could be told that they couldn't eat in the same restaurants, sleep in the same participate. The Attorneys General of the states requiring or permitting segregation in public education will also be permitted to appear as amici curiae **("friends of the court")** upon request to do so by September 15, 1954, and submission of briefs by October 1, 1954.

It is so ordered. ★

hotels, or even drink from the same water fountains, but still experience an equally good life. It was this ruling that told black people they had to move to the back of the bus.

The Supreme Court finally agreed to hear *Brown v. Board of Education* in 1952. The case was then re-argued in 1953 before finally being decided on in 1954. It goes without saying that the end of "separate but equal" was many years in the making. Imagine having to wait two years for something that you really, really want. Not easy, right? Now imagine having to wait over 100 years. Lawyers had been arguing for equal schooling for black children since 1849; to say that this decision was a long time coming would be an understatement.

Speaking of long, the opinion written by Warren is pretty long. The text included here actually comes from page 494(!) of the 1954 decision. A case with such huge historical implications deserved this many pages, though. Warren, in laying out the court's decision and the reasons for that decision, was able to sum up the long-lasting effect that segregation has when he stated that keeping these kids separate "may affect their hearts and minds in a way unlikely ever to be undone." This really makes clear just how serious the case was and how much was at stake. Children were being hurt, and the hurt wasn't ever going to go away because it was having such an impact on their self-image. When separated, the students were not only aware that they were getting less, many of them felt they *deserved* less because they were *worth* less. Warren's concern was that this feeling of inferiority would last throughout each child's lifetime. He worried that it would be hard for them to be successful adults if the education they received was of a lesser quality than the education received by people who they'd be competing against for admission to college and jobs. Based on the testimony they heard, the justices were able to decide that "separate but equal" was unjust and illegal.

Often times, the Supreme Court will hear cases that have to do with past decisions made by the three branches of government. Basically, the court is interested in righting any wrongs that are impacting American citizens, and one of the things that worried Warren was the idea that the American government had actually supported the idea of "separate but equal" with the *Plessy v. Ferguson* decision. He wrote that "Segregation with the sanction of law, therefore, has a tendency to [retard] the educational and mental development of negro children," and that this is why it's so important to have integrated, or mixed, schools. There are two points worth thinking about here. One is the idea that separation was, up until now, allowed because it was legal. Not only did black parents have to wonder about why their children were receiving less of an education than white children, they had to wonder why the school districts wanted to run their schools this way, why the towns and states wanted to allow it, and why the

Supreme Court said it was legal. The second thing worth thinking about is that the development of black children had been retarded, or severely slowed down, by this. It's like stunted growth, but of the mind. These are just two reasons why Warren allowed *Brown v. Board of Education* to be argued before his Supreme Court and why he ruled on it the way that he did.

You might wonder what school districts tried to do after this ruling. Well, some districts bussed kids from one neighborhood to another, so as to mix them all together—Boston is the most famous example of this. Magnet schools, meant to "draw" kids from different towns and neighborhoods to a certain school, were another way that government officials and educators tried to integrate students. Although bussing is not as popular as it once was, the number of magnet schools, especially in cities, is growing at a rapid pace. The spirit of *Brown v. Board of Education* is still alive and well, 50-plus years after Marshall had his big day in court.

There have actually been three decisions involving *Brown v. Board of Education*. The first, from 1954, is the most famous. It was the initial court ruling that determined that segregation in public education is unconstitutional and is known as Brown I. In 1955, the court revisited the case in an effort to require that school districts make all of the necessary changes "with all deliberate speed." This decision is known as Brown II. Finally, in 1979 three attorneys in Topeka asked the court to decide if the school board had really put an end to segregation like they were supposed to. This is known as Brown III.

But back to 1954 now. Warren knew that it would be hard to get all of the states, towns, and school districts to comply with, or obey, the Supreme Court's ruling. In the final paragraph of the excerpt, he invited the attorneys general of each state to let the court know about the problems they thought they might have with integrating their schools. The Latin phrase used to describe their role was *amici curiae,* which literally translates to "friends of the court." The attorneys general, who were in charge of all legal issues in their states, were being asked to help out by providing information that would make the change from segregation to integration go much more smoothly. It was also Warren's attempt to short-circuit any complaining the states might do and to ensure that his decision actually led to significant improvements. Despite "all deliberate speed" and *amici curiae,* the National Guard still had to escort students into certain schools. Despite this resistance, it's to Warren's credit, as well as to the credit of the NAACP, Thurgood Marshall, Oliver Brown, and all of the other families involved, that this case eventually led to significant improvements. The era of separate but equal was no more. ★

# Who Would Write It Today?

If there were to be a class action involving individual rights today, the decision would be written by Chief Justice John Roberts. You and your friends might use the Internet to gather support from students across the country in an attempt to bring your case before the Supreme Court. That case might involve putting a limit on homework, but it's doubtful any court, let alone the Supreme Court, would hear that case! But if it were something with more substance, something like challenging the voting age of 18, and arguing for 16 years of age, they might decide to hear the case. If so, somebody would have to write the decision and similar to Chief Justice Earl Warren's opinion in *Brown v. Board of Education* it would probably be Chief Justice John Roberts.

## PRESIDENT
# JOHN F. KENNEDY'S INAUGURAL ADDRESS

## JANUARY 1961

**In 50 Words or Less!** In 1961, John F. Kennedy became America's youngest president. He understood the serious responsibilities facing him and addressed many of them on the day he was sworn in as our 35th president. In particular, he used his speech to discuss his hopes for ending the Cold War and poverty.

# PRESIDENT JOHN F. KENNEDY'S INAUGURAL ADDRESS

Vice President Johnson, Mr. Speaker, Mr. Chief Justice, President Eisenhower, Vice President Nixon, President Truman, Reverend Clergy, fellow citizens:

We observe today not a victory of party, but a celebration of freedom—symbolizing an end, as well as a beginning—signifying renewal, as well as change. For I have sworn before you and Almighty God the same solemn **(serious)** oath our forebears prescribed nearly a century and three-quarters ago.

The world is very different now. **For man holds in his mortal hands the power to abolish (eliminate) all forms of human poverty and all forms of human life.** And yet the same revolutionary beliefs for which our forebears fought are still at issue around the globe—the belief that the rights of man come not from the generosity of the state, but from the hand of God.

We dare not forget today that we are the heirs of that first revolution. Let the word go forth from this time and place, to friend and foe alike, that the torch has been passed to a new generation of Americans—born in this century, tempered by war, disciplined by a hard and bitter peace, proud of our ancient heritage, and unwilling to witness or

**SUMMARY:** It should be no surprise that as the dates of these historical texts get closer and closer to the present day they become easier and easier to understand. This isn't to say that the words are any less important. They may not be difficult to read, but they're certainly as deep and meaningful as anything that came before.

John F. Kennedy was one of America's most eloquent presidents. His words were always deep and meaningful. Although Ted Sorenson and John Kenneth Galbraith advised him on his inaugural address, it has been proven that most of the credit should be given to Kennedy. You might think this isn't very important, but historians like to know when someone should get credited or just be acknowledged for helping out. Also, when you read the speech, you'll see that Kennedy's command of the language and the way he uses turn of phrase to get his point across deserves recognition. In this speech, his main points revolve around protecting liberty and fighting tyranny, and the thoughts he had in his head and the skill with which he delivered them must have filled Americans with great confidence in their new leader. Here are five examples:

permit the slow undoing of those human rights to which this nation has always been committed, and to which we are committed today at home and around the world.

**Let every nation know, whether it wishes us well or ill, that we shall pay any price, bear any burden, meet any hardship, support any friend, oppose any foe, to assure the survival and the success of liberty.**

This much we pledge—and more.

To those old allies whose cultural and spiritual origins we share, we pledge the loyalty of faithful friends. United there is little we cannot do in a host of cooperative ventures. Divided there is little we can do—for we dare not meet a powerful challenge at odds and split asunder **(into separate pieces)**.

To those new states whom we welcome to the ranks of the free, we pledge our word that one form of colonial control shall not have passed away merely to be replaced by a far more iron tyranny **(domination)**. We shall not always expect to find them supporting our view. But we shall always hope to find them strongly supporting their own freedom—and to **remember that, in the past, those who foolishly sought power by riding the back of the tiger ended up inside.**

To those people in the huts and villages of half the globe struggling to break the bonds of mass misery, we pledge our best efforts to help

"If a free society cannot help the many who are poor, it cannot save the few who are rich."

"For only when our arms are sufficient beyond doubt can we be certain beyond doubt that they will never be employed."

"Let us never negotiate out of fear, but let us never fear to negotiate."

" . . . and bring the absolute power to destroy other nations under the absolute control of all nations."

"And so, my fellow Americans, ask not what your country can do for you; ask what you can do for your country."

That last line is one you've probably heard before. It's the most famous part of Kennedy's speech and sums up his opinion that, in order to win the Cold War, every American must contribute. Kennedy was saying that he couldn't ensure peace or protect freedom all by himself. He was going to need some help. This included help from the Soviets who he hoped would soon see the error of their ways.

The Cold War was a competition between the United States and the Soviet Union, but the talk became tough when the competition began to involve more and more atomic bombs. Kennedy recognized the responsibility that was in his hands

them help themselves, for whatever period is required—not because the Communists may be doing it, not because we seek their votes, but because it is right. **If a free society cannot help the many who are poor, it cannot save the few who are rich.**

To our sister republics south of our border, we offer a special pledge: to convert our good words into good deeds, in a new alliance for progress, to assist free men and free governments in casting off the chains of poverty. But this peaceful revolution of hope cannot become the prey of hostile powers. Let all our neighbors know that we shall join with them to oppose aggression or subversion **(rebellion)** anywhere in the Americas. **And let every other power know that this hemisphere intends to remain the master of its own house.**

To that world assembly of sovereign **(independent)** states, the United Nations, our last best hope in an age where the instruments of war have far outpaced the instruments of peace, we renew our pledge of support—to prevent it from becoming merely a forum for invective **(criticism)**, to strengthen its shield of the new and the weak, and to enlarge the area in which its writ may run.

Finally, to those nations who would make themselves our adversary, we offer not a pledge but a request: that both sides begin anew the quest for peace, before the dark powers of destruction unleashed by science engulf all humanity in planned or accidental self-destruction.

when he said that man has the power to abolish "all forms of human life," but he also wanted the Soviets to know that he meant business: " . . . we shall pay any price, bear any burden, meet any hardship, support any friend, oppose any foe, to assure the survival and the success of liberty." And he meant survival, literally. During Kennedy's presidency, the Soviets tried to put their missiles on the island of Cuba, 90 miles south of Florida, which means right in America's backyard. The Cuban Missile Crisis really forced Kennedy to live up to the words of his inaugural address. Fortunately, the Soviets were convinced that he would walk the walk and not just talk the talk, and the ships carrying those missiles never made it to Cuba.

In addressing those nations that had been our friends in the past—the Soviets among them as they'd been our allies during World War II—Kennedy recalled Lincoln's Biblical reference "a house divided against itself cannot stand" with his, "United there is little we cannot do in a host of cooperative ventures. Divided there is little we can do . . . " Later, he states, "Let both sides explore what problems unite us instead of belaboring those problems which divide us." This was his way of asking the Soviets for their cooperation. He also cleverly refers to the splitting of atoms (which is what causes an atomic explosion) when he says "powerful challenge at odds and *split* asunder."

**We dare not tempt them with weakness. For only when our arms are sufficient beyond doubt can we be certain beyond doubt that they will never be employed.**

But neither can two great and powerful groups of nations take comfort from our present course—both sides overburdened by the cost of modern weapons, both rightly alarmed by the steady spread of the deadly atom, yet both racing to alter that uncertain balance of terror that stays (delays) the hand of mankind's final war.

So let us begin anew—remembering on both sides that civility (courtesy) is not a sign of weakness, and sincerity is always subject to proof. **Let us never negotiate out of fear, but let us never fear to negotiate.**

Let both sides explore what problems unite us instead of belaboring (overstressing) those problems which divide us.

Let both sides, for the first time, formulate serious and precise proposals for the inspection and control of arms, and bring the absolute power to destroy other nations under the absolute control of all nations.

Let both sides seek to invoke the wonders of science instead of its terrors. Together let us explore the stars, conquer the deserts, eradicate (get rid of) disease, tap the ocean depths, and encourage the arts and commerce.

Kennedy easily goes from historical/Biblical references to nuclear science references to the lessons of fables. Although it's easy to figure out what he meant when he said to remember that "... those who foolishly sought power by riding the back of the tiger ended up inside."—in other words, they ended up as dinner!—it's still a phrase worth noting. At some point during his travels around the world, Kennedy must have heard the tiger quote as part of some sort of tribal story, and there it was, re-emerging to bring home a point in his inaugural speech.

Perhaps because of his travels, Kennedy was very interested in ending world poverty. (Who knows how much he could've accomplished had there been no Cold War and no assassin's bullet?) He coined the phrase "third world nation" and, in the same year as his inaugural address, authorized funding for the Peace Corps. He felt that communist-socialist governments were keeping poor people poor but also that Americans had a responsibility to the global community. Kennedy reminded Americans, "If a free society cannot help the many who are poor, it cannot save the few who are rich." He even referred to the improvements he hoped to see in poor countries as a "peaceful revolution." Kennedy, the historian, is making reference to the Monroe Doctrine and to protecting countries in our hemisphere from outside interference. Today, Cuba remains the only communist country in the western hemisphere.

Let both sides unite to heed, in all corners of the earth, the command of Isaiah—to "undo the heavy burdens, and [to] let the oppressed go free."

**And, if a beachhead of cooperation may push back the jungle of suspicion, let both sides join in creating a new endeavor—not a new balance of power, but a new world of law—where the strong are just, and the weak secure, and the peace preserved.**

All this will not be finished in the first one hundred days. Nor will it be finished in the first one thousand days; nor in the life of this Administration; nor even perhaps in our lifetime on this planet. But let us begin.

In your hands, my fellow citizens, more than mine, will rest the final success or failure of our course. Since this country was founded, each generation of Americans has been summoned to give testimony to its national loyalty. The graves of young Americans who answered the call to service surround the globe.

Now the trumpet summons us again—not as a call to bear arms, though arms we need—not as a call to battle, though embattled we are—but a call to bear the burden of a long twilight struggle, year in and year out, "rejoicing in hope; patient in tribulation," a struggle against the common enemies of man: tyranny, poverty, disease, and war itself.

Kennedy also mentions the United Nations (UN) and that this "assembly of sovereign states" is " . . . our last best hope in an age where the instruments of war have far outpaced the instruments of peace . . . " He was a world leader unafraid to drop bombs, but it was his sincere hope that he wouldn't have to. Just as his fellow Americans—and his rival Soviets—had a responsibility to the world, so too did the UN.

The Cold War was certainly a competition between two countries, but even more specifically Kennedy saw it as race. When the Soviets launched Sputnik, he charged NASA with putting a man on the moon, thus starting the space race. (His "Together let us explore the stars . . . " was a bit of a false statement.) Far more dangerous was the arms race that lasted until the fall of communism when Ronald Reagan was president. Kennedy used that old turn of phrase trick again when he stated, "For only when our arms are sufficient beyond doubt can we be certain beyond doubt that they will never be employed." We would keep stockpiling bombs, he promised, until the Soviets knew we could do more destruction than them. The problem ended up being that they matched us bomb for bomb so that during the 1960s, 1970s, and 1980s billions and billions of dollars were spent trying to be the biggest bully on the block.

Can we forge against these enemies a grand and global alliance, North and South, East and West, that can assure a more fruitful life for all mankind? Will you join in that historic effort?

In the long history of the world, only a few generations have been granted the role of defending freedom in its hour of maximum danger. I do not shrink from this responsibility—I welcome it. I do not believe that any of us would exchange places with any other people or any other generation. The energy, the faith, the devotion which we bring to this endeavor will light our country and all who serve it. And the glow from that fire can truly light the world.

**And so, my fellow Americans, ask not what your country can do for you; ask what you can do for your country.**

My fellow citizens of the world, ask not what America will do for you, but what together we can do for the freedom of man.

Finally, whether you are citizens of America or citizens of the world, ask of us here the same high standards of strength and sacrifice which we ask of you. With a good conscience **(sense of right and wrong)** our only sure reward, with history the final judge of our deeds, let us go forth to lead the land we love, asking His blessing and His help, but knowing that here on earth God's work must truly be our own. ★

If you're ever asked to name one emotion that sums up the Cold War era, *suspicion* might be a good one. Kennedy said he hoped that through cooperation, the United States and the Soviet Union might " . . . push back the jungle of suspicion, . . . " but this never happened. Not until the Soviet Union fell apart were opposing leaders able to have open, honest conversations. Russia and its satellite countries are still trying to figure out, today, how to make democracy and capitalism work. Kennedy would be pleased to know that America is still going strong, but his humanitarian side would be sad to know that so many people living in the former Soviet Union are still living in poverty. ★

---

In Addition . . . Robert Frost, the famous American poet, called Kennedy's inauguration speech "A turning point in modern history."

---

# What Others Have Said

Lyndon B. Johnson, who became president when Kennedy was assassinated, used some turn of phrase of his own when he said, "John F. Kennedy was the victim of the hate that was a part of our country. It is a disease that occupies the minds of the few but brings danger to the many."

PRESIDENT RONALD REAGAN'S

# REMARKS AT THE BRANDENBURG GATE

## JUNE 1987

**In 50 Words or Less!** In 1987, President Reagan gave a speech as he stood before the Berlin Wall. He summed up the Cold War, then described his hope for a future of greater freedom and fewer bombs. His speech marked the beginning of the end of communism, the Soviet Union, and the Cold War.

# PRESIDENT RONALD REAGAN'S REMARKS AT THE BRANDENBURG GATE

Thank you very much.

Chancellor Kohl, Governing Mayor Diepgen, ladies and gentlemen: Twenty-four years ago, President John F. Kennedy visited Berlin, speaking to the people of this city and the world at the City Hall. Well, since then two other presidents have come, each in his turn, to Berlin. And today I, myself, make my second visit to your city.

We come to Berlin, we American presidents, because it's our duty to speak, in this place, of freedom. But I must confess, we're drawn here by other things as well: **by the feeling of history in this city, more than 500 years older than our own nation;** by the beauty of the Grunewald and the Tiergarten; most of all, by your courage and determination. Perhaps the composer Paul Lincke understood something about American presidents. You see, like so many presidents before me, I come here today because wherever I go, whatever I do: Ich hab noch einen Koffer in Berlin. [I still have a suitcase in Berlin.]

Our gathering today is being broadcast throughout Western Europe and North America. I understand that it is being seen and heard as well in the East. **To those listening throughout Eastern Europe, a special word: Although I cannot be with you, I address my remarks to you**

**SUMMARY:** In 1945, when World War II was just about over and the Cold War just about to begin, leaders from the United States, Great Britain, and Soviet Union met at a vacation resort in the Soviet city of Yalta. Franklin D. Roosevelt, Winston Churchill, and Josef Stalin gathered to peacefully make plans for the postwar world. With so much at stake, though, in terms of territory, resources, and money, the seeds of dispute were planted and over the coming years, the Soviets and the United States would confront one another on their political (communism versus democracy) and economic (socialism versus capitalism) differences again and again and again. But in 1945, the biggest problem facing the countries was deciding how severely Germany should be punished and how its land should be divided between the Allies. Walking away from Yalta, who could've predicted that all of these differences of opinion would last until 1991?

World War II officially ended a week after the United States dropped two atomic bombs on Japan. The bombs were meant to deliver a very loud ultimatum. Not only did America want to send the Japanese a message (that their efforts would never be enough to beat us), the hope was that the Soviet

**JUNE 1987**

just as surely as to those standing here before me. For I join you, as I join your fellow countrymen in the West, in this firm, this unalterable belief: **Es gibt nur ein Berlin. [There is only one Berlin.]**

Behind me stands a wall that encircles the free sectors of this city, part of a vast system of barriers that divides the entire continent of Europe. From the Baltic, south, those barriers cut across Germany in a gash of barbed wire, concrete, dog runs, and guard towers. Farther south, there may be no visible, no obvious wall. But there remain armed guards and checkpoints all the same—still a restriction on the right to travel, still an instrument to impose upon ordinary men and women the will of a totalitarian **(authoritarian)** state. Yet it is here in Berlin where the wall emerges most clearly; here, cutting across your city, where the news photo and the television screen have imprinted this brutal division of a continent upon the mind of the world. **Standing before the Brandenburg Gate, every man is a German, separated from his fellow men. Every man is a Berliner, forced to look upon a scar.**

President von Weizsacker has said, "The German question is open as long as the Brandenburg Gate is closed." Today I say: **As long as the gate is closed, as long as this scar of a wall is permitted to stand, it is not the German question alone that remains open, but the question of freedom for all mankind.** Yet I do not come here to lament **(mourn).** For I find in Berlin a message of hope, even in the shadow of this wall, a message of triumph.

Union would get the message, too. They heard us, but rather than back down, they decided to try and one-up us. The more atomic bombs we built, the more atomic bombs they built. By the time the Cold War ended, Roosevelt and Stalin had been replaced by Ronald Reagan and Mikhail Gorbachev, and the two countries had enough bombs to blow up the entire world—again and again and again! Because of this, the Cold War was a scary time for many of the world's citizens. Even kids understood that with the push of a button the world could be destroyed.

When World War II ended, Germany was split in two, including its capital city of Berlin. East Germany (and East Berlin) was communist and an ally of the Soviets. West Germany (and West Berlin) was an ally of countries like the United States and Great Britain. The Berlin Wall kept the citizens of Berlin apart from one another—people had family members living on the other side that they couldn't ever see. At best, they could stand on opposite sides and talk to one another *over* the wall. But in 1990, the two Germanies reunited and one year later, the Soviet Union collapsed, thus ending the Cold War. In the years leading up to these two monumental events, President Ronald Reagan played an important role in fighting communism and in trying to find peaceful answers to the continuing problems of Soviet versus U.S. and of East versus West.

In this season of spring in 1945, the people of Berlin emerged from their air-raid shelters to find devastation. Thousands of miles away, the people of the United States reached out to help. And in 1947 Secretary of State—as you've been told—George Marshall announced the creation of what would become known as the Marshall Plan. Speaking precisely 40 years ago this month, he said: "Our policy is directed not against any country or doctrine, but against hunger, poverty, desperation, and chaos."

In the Reichstag a few moments ago, I saw a display commemorating **(honoring)** this 40th anniversary of the Marshall Plan. I was struck by the sign on a burnt-out, gutted structure that was being rebuilt. I understand that Berliners of my own generation can remember seeing signs like it dotted throughout the western sectors of the city. The sign read simply: "The Marshall Plan is helping here to strengthen the free world." A strong, free world in the West, that dream became real. Japan rose from ruin to become an economic giant. Italy, France, Belgium—virtually every nation in Western Europe saw political and economic rebirth; the European Community was founded.

In West Germany and here in Berlin, there took place an economic miracle, the Wirtschaftswunder. Adenauer, Erhard, Reuter, and other leaders understood the practical importance of liberty—that **just as truth can flourish only when the journalist is given freedom of speech, so prosperity can come about only when the farmer and businessman enjoy economic freedom.** The German leaders reduced

When Reagan stood before the Brandenburg Gate in 1987, people on both sides of the Berlin Wall were able to hear his speech. He was addressing the people of West Berlin, but wanted the East Berliners to hear his message, too. Reagan suspected that many of them couldn't wait for the day the wall came down and they could begin to enjoy freedom, democracy, and capitalism.

Speaking in Berlin 24 years after President Kennedy paid his visit, Reagan combined diplomacy with might, and patriotism with a worldly perspective. In a nutshell, he gave a great speech! If you were to fly over Berlin at that time, you would see the Berlin Wall snaking through the city like a scar, and this is an image Reagan put in everyone's head when he said that all Berliners were being "forced to look upon a scar" and also when he stated, "As long as the gate is closed, as long as this scar of a wall is permitted to stand, it is not the German question alone that remains open, but the question of freedom for all mankind." Germany was an important stepping-stone to replacing all communist governments with democratically elected governments, and to replacing all socialist economies with capitalist economies. In short, socialism means that the government controls all of the resources, companies, and workers. There's supposed to be equal wealth among all of the people. On the flip side, in socialist economies, the government is allowed to tell you what job you'll have. In capitalist tariffs **(taxes on internationally traded goods)**, expanded free trade, lowered taxes. From 1950 to 1960 alone, the standard of living in West Germany and Berlin doubled.

Where four decades ago there was rubble, today in West Berlin there is the greatest industrial output of any city in Germany—busy office blocks, fine homes and apartments, proud avenues, and the spreading lawns of parkland. Where a city's culture seemed to have been destroyed, today there are two great universities, orchestras and an opera, countless theaters, and museums. Where there was want, today there's abundance—food, clothing, automobiles—the wonderful goods of the Ku'damm. **From devastation, from utter ruin, you Berliners have, in freedom, rebuilt a city that once again ranks as one of the greatest on earth.** The Soviets may have had other plans. But my friends, there were a few things the Soviets didn't count on—Berliner Herz, Berliner Humor, ja, und Berliner Schnauze. [Berliner heart, Berliner humor, yes, and a Berliner Schnauze.]

In the 1950s, Khrushchev **(the Soviet premier)** predicted: "We will bury you." But in the West today, we see a free world that has achieved a level of prosperity **(wealth)** and well-being unprecedented in all human history. In the Communist world, we see failure, technological backwardness, declining standards of health, even want of the most basic kind—too little food. Even today, the Soviet Union still cannot feed itself. After these four decades, then, there stands before the entire world one great and inescapable conclusion: **Freedom leads to**

economies, you're free to do whatever you want; to be as rich as you want or as poor as you want; to work in a coffee shop or go to med school to become a doctor. Entrepreneurs in a capitalist economy are free to start up their own businesses. There's the risk of losing all of the money that you invest in your business, but there's also the chance that you'll be very successful. People living in socialist economies don't really have the option of being entrepreneurs. Reagan wanted everyone in the world to have all the same choices that his fellow Americans had, from deciding on a job to electing government officials.

Reagan referred to the success that Japan experienced in the years after World War II. Japan had been a fierce enemy, but it accepted our help and welcomed our democracy and capitalism into its nation, even letting American general, Douglas MacArthur, write its new constitution! Japan focused its economy on technology and automobiles and quickly recovered from the devastation of the war. Germany, or at least the eastern half of Germany, didn't have that chance because it was controlled by the Soviets. It made Reagan sad to think of how powerful Germany had once been and how now, under this division of east and west, the country was suffering. He offered America's help if only the Soviets would open the Brandenburg Gate; if only Mr. Gorbachev would "tear down this wall!" This is the most famous line not only of Reagan's speech but also of his eight years as president.

prosperity. Freedom replaces the ancient hatreds among the nations with comity **(social harmony)** and peace. Freedom is the victor.

And now the Soviets themselves may, in a limited way, be coming to understand the importance of freedom. We hear much from Moscow about a new policy of reform and openness. Some political prisoners have been released. Certain foreign news broadcasts are no longer being jammed. Some economic enterprises have been permitted to operate with greater freedom from state control.

Are these the beginnings of profound changes in the Soviet state? Or are they token gestures, intended to raise false hopes in the West, or to strengthen the Soviet system without changing it? We welcome change and openness; for we believe that freedom and security go together, that the advance of human liberty can only strengthen the cause of world peace. **There is one sign the Soviets can make that would be unmistakable, that would advance dramatically the cause of freedom and peace.**

General Secretary Gorbachev, if you seek peace, if you seek prosperity for the Soviet Union and Eastern Europe, if you seek liberalization: Come here to this gate! Mr. Gorbachev, open this gate! **Mr. Gorbachev, tear down this wall!**

I understand the fear of war and the pain of division that afflict **(upset)** this continent—and I pledge to you my country's efforts to help overcome these burdens. To be sure, we in the West must resist

Halfway through his remarks, Reagan shifted gears and spoke about the arms race that characterized the Cold War. As both countries added more and more missiles to their arsenal, the world became a more dangerous place to live. But you know how it is: Once you open your mouth and start saying you won't back down, you can't very well back down, can you? Well, that's how Reagan felt. The United States just couldn't back down. Rather than adding even more nuclear weapons to our stockpile, though, he had a new idea. He'd counteract the efforts of the Soviets with a defense system known as the Strategic Defense Initiative that promised to "not target populations, but shield them." Reagan's speech is markedly balanced between tough talk and hope for peace. He was really asking the Soviets to recognize that America had everything under control, that we couldn't be outdone, and that it was time for the Soviets to come back to the table and negotiate.

Recalling that well-spoken president of 24 years before, Reagan used some turn of phrase of his own when he stated, "East and West do not mistrust each other because we are armed; we are armed because we mistrust each other." Although his hope that there would be greater trust is still a work in progress, his prediction of a technological revolution in industrialized nations was really right on. Cell phones were as big as a brick back then, and more people had cassette-playing Walkmen than compact disc-playing Discmen. Science

Soviet expansion. So we must maintain defenses of unassailable **(unquestionable)** strength. Yet we seek peace; so we must strive to reduce arms on both sides.

Beginning 10 years ago, the Soviets challenged the Western alliance with a grave new threat, hundreds of new and more deadly SS-20 nuclear missiles, capable of striking every capital in Europe. The Western alliance responded by committing itself to a counter-deployment unless the Soviets agreed to negotiate a better solution; namely, the elimination of such weapons on both sides. For many months, the Soviets refused to bargain in earnestness **(seriousness)**. As the alliance, in turn, prepared to go forward with its counter-deployment, there were difficult days—days of protests like those during my 1982 visit to this city—and the Soviets later walked away from the table.

But through it all, the alliance held firm. And I invite those who protested then—I invite those who protest today—to mark this fact: Because we remained strong, the Soviets came back to the table. **And because we remained strong, today we have within reach the possibility, not merely of limiting the growth of arms, but of eliminating, for the first time, an entire class of nuclear weapons from the face of the earth.**

As I speak, NATO ministers are meeting in Iceland to review the progress of our proposals for eliminating these weapons. At the talks in Geneva, we have also proposed deep cuts in strategic offensive fiction writers of the 1980s couldn't have envisioned the iPod, but Reagan saw what was coming. He knew that the wealthy countries were only going to get wealthier with their new technology and that the poorer, communist countries would fall even further behind. Fortunately, these days you'll find as many cell phones and MP3 players in Russia and Germany as in the United States! This would not be the case had communism been allowed to continue.

Even as Reagan spoke of the future, he looked back at the long history of Berlin when he noted that this was "the 750th anniversary of this city." What a perfect time, he hinted, for beginning a new era. This era, he offered, could include youth exchanges and international athletic competitions like the Olympics. It was in Berlin, after all, that Jesse Owens had disproved Hitler's belief, as the Nazi leader looked on, that a black man could never defeat a white man. Reagan wanted all of the countries involved to return to competition of a healthier nature. During the 1980s, America boycotted the Olympics in Moscow, and then the Soviets boycotted the Olympics in Los Angeles. It was time for the protesting to end and for everyone to gather again on the fields of play.

Toward the end of his remarks, Reagan recognized the people that had gathered to protest. Employing the political sense that was evident throughout his presidency, Reagan asked these weapons. And the Western allies have likewise made far-reaching proposals to reduce the danger of conventional war and to place a total ban on chemical weapons.

While we pursue these arms reductions, I pledge to you that we will maintain the capacity to deter **(prevent)** Soviet aggression at any level at which it might occur. **And in cooperation with many of our allies, the United States is pursuing the Strategic Defense Initiative—research to base deterrence not on the threat of offensive retaliation, but on defenses that truly defend; on systems, in short, that will not target populations, but shield them.** By these means we seek to increase the safety of Europe and all the world. But we must remember a crucial fact: **East and West do not mistrust each other because we are armed; we are armed because we mistrust each other.** And our differences are not about weapons but about liberty. When President Kennedy spoke at the City Hall those 24 years ago, freedom was encircled, Berlin was under siege. And today, despite all the pressures upon this city, Berlin stands secure in its liberty. And freedom itself is transforming the globe.

In the Philippines, in South and Central America, democracy has been given a rebirth. Throughout the Pacific, free markets are working miracle after miracle of economic growth. In the industrialized nations, a technological revolution is taking place—a revolution marked by rapid, dramatic advances in computers and telecommunications.

West Germans who were lucky enough to have a democratic government if they thought they'd be allowed to demonstrate like this if they were living under a communist government? The answer, all in attendance knew, was no. With that, Reagan concluded his remarks. Three years later, Germany (and Berlin) was reunited, and one year later, the Soviet Union ceased to be the communist superpower that had opposed us throughout the long Cold War. In 1992, these countries and all of their allies sent athletes to participate in the Olympics at Albertville. A record number of Olympians, and nations, participated just as Reagan had hoped it would be. ★

In Addition . . . Just like John F. Kennedy, Ronald Reagan suffered at the hands of an assassin. Fortunately though, Reagan survived. John Hinckley Jr.'s motive had nothing to do with the cold war. Found to be insane, Hinckley had decided that by killing Reagan, the actress Jodi Foster would notice him and fall in love with him. As Reagan was wheeled into the operating room to have the bullets removed, he joked, "I hope you're all Republicans." It was then that everyone knew the president would be just fine.

In Europe, only one nation and those it controls refuse to join the community of freedom. Yet in this age of redoubled economic growth, of information and innovation, the Soviet Union faces a choice: It must make fundamental changes, or it will become obsolete **(out-dated)**.

Today thus represents a moment of hope. **We in the West stand ready to cooperate with the East to promote true openness, to break down barriers that separate people, to create a safe, freer world. And surely there is no better place than Berlin, the meeting place of East and West, to make a start.** Free people of Berlin: Today, as in the past, the United States stands for the strict observance and full implementation of all parts of the Four Power Agreement of 1971. Let us use this occasion, **the 750th anniversary of this city,** to usher in a new era, to seek a still fuller, richer life for the Berlin of the future. Together, let us maintain and develop the ties between the Federal Republic and the Western sectors of Berlin, which is permitted by the 1971 agreement.

And I invite Mr. Gorbachev: Let us work to bring the Eastern and Western parts of the city closer together, so that all the inhabitants of all Berlin can enjoy the benefits that come with life in one of the great cities of the world.

To open Berlin still further to all Europe, East and West, let us expand the vital air access to this city, finding ways of making commercial air service to Berlin more convenient, more comfortable, and more economical. We look to the day when West Berlin can become one of the chief aviation hubs in all central Europe.

With our French and British partners, the United States is prepared to help bring international meetings to Berlin. It would be only fitting for Berlin to serve as the site of United Nations meetings, or world conferences on human rights and arms control or other issues that call for international cooperation.

**There is no better way to establish hope for the future than to enlighten young minds, and we would be honored to sponsor summer youth exchanges, cultural events, and other programs for young Berliners from the East.** Our French and British friends, I'm certain, will do the same. And it's my hope that an authority can be found in East Berlin to sponsor visits from young people of the Western sectors.

One final proposal, one close to my heart: Sport represents a source of enjoyment and ennoblement (giving people their dignity), and you may have noted that the Republic of Korea—South Korea—has offered to permit certain events of the 1988 Olympics to take place in the North. International sports competitions of all kinds could take place in both parts of this city. **And what better way to demonstrate to the world the openness of this city than to offer in some future year to hold the Olympic games here in Berlin, East and West?** In these four decades, as I have said, you

Berliners have built a great city. You've done so in spite of threats—the Soviet attempts to impose the East-mark, the blockade. Today the city thrives in spite of the challenges implicit **(contained)** in the very presence of this wall. What keeps you here? Certainly there's a great deal to be said for your fortitude, for your defiant courage. But I believe there's something deeper, something that involves Berlin's whole look and feel and way of life—not mere sentiment **(emotion)**. No one could live long in Berlin without being completely disabused of illusions **(able to see and understand the truth)**. Something instead, that has seen the difficulties of life in Berlin but chose to accept them, that continues to build this good and proud city in contrast to a surrounding totalitarian presence that refuses to release human energies or aspirations. Something that speaks with a powerful voice of affirmation, that says yes to this city, yes to the future, yes to freedom. In a word, I would submit that what keeps you in Berlin is love—love both profound **(thoughtful)** and abiding **(surviving)**.

Perhaps this gets to the root of the matter, to the most fundamental distinction of all between East and West. The totalitarian world produces backwardness because it does such violence to the spirit, thwarting the human impulse to create, to enjoy, to worship. The totalitarian world finds even symbols of love and of worship an affront **(insult)**. Years ago, before the East Germans began rebuilding their churches, they erected a secular structure: the television tower at Alexander Platz. Virtually ever since, the authorities have been working to correct what they view as the tower's one major flaw, treating the glass sphere at the top with paints and chemicals of every kind. Yet even today when the sun strikes that sphere—that sphere that towers over all Berlin—the light makes the sign of the cross. There in Berlin, like the city itself, symbols of love, symbols of worship, cannot be suppressed **(covered up)**.

As I looked out a moment ago from the Reichstag, that embodiment of German unity, I noticed words crudely spray-painted upon the wall, perhaps by a young Berliner: "This wall will fall. Beliefs become reality." Yes, across Europe, this wall will fall. For it cannot withstand faith; it cannot withstand truth. The wall cannot withstand freedom.

**And I would like, before I close, to say one word. I have read, and I have been questioned since I've been here about certain demonstrations against my coming. And I would like to say just one thing, and to those who demonstrate so. I wonder if they have ever asked themselves that if they should have the kind of government they apparently seek, no one would ever be able to do what they're doing again.**

Thank you and God bless you all. ★

"Remarks on East–West Relations at the Brandenburg Gate in West Berlin June 12, 1987." The Public Papers of President Ronald W. Reagan. Ronald Reagan Presidential Library. *www.reagan.utexas.edu.*

# What Others Have Said

Mikhail Gorbachev, upon hearing the news of Reagan's death in 2004, said, "Reagan was a statesman who, despite all disagreements that existed between our countries at the time, displayed foresight and determination to meet our proposals halfway and change our relations for the better, stop the nuclear race, start scrapping nuclear weapons, and arrange normal relations between our countries . . . Reagan, whom many considered extremely rightist, dared to make these steps, and this is his most important deed."

★ ★ ★ ★ ★ ★ ★ ★ ★ ★ ★ ★ ★ ★ ★ ★ ★ ★ ★ ★ ★ ★ ★ ★ ★ ★ ★ ★ ★

APPENDIX:

# THE PEOPLE BEHIND THE HISTORICAL TEXTS

★ ★ ★ ★ ★ ★ ★ ★ ★ ★ ★ ★ ★ ★ ★ ★ ★ ★ ★ ★ ★ ★ ★ ★ ★ ★ ★ ★ ★

**Summary:** Some historical documents are easy to trace—they were released to the public by the author in the form of a book, court opinion, song, or speech. Others, however, aren't so easy to credit. This section is a chance for you to find out more about the authors included in the book as well as those people generally *acknowledged* as having done most of the writing (or creating or editing) of the specific historical text. It's important that good work be recognized, don't you think?

# THE MAYFLOWER COMPACT

While there's no absolute proof, it's believed that **William Bradford** (1590–1657) wrote the original draft of the Mayflower Compact. He composed this document while the Mayflower crossed the Atlantic Ocean, first putting quill to parchment, then presenting his work to the other men for suggestions, and then, finally, asking for approval in the form of their signatures.

After the first winter in Plymouth, the Pilgrims unanimously elected Bradford to be their governor, and he held that position for more than 30 years. He wrote a history of the Pilgrims' experiences, titled *History of Plimoth Plantation*, a book that wasn't published until the mid-1800s but is still considered an important primary source of information about the Plymouth Colony. He also wrote three other books.

# INTRODUCTION TO THOMAS PAINE'S *COMMON SENSE, THIRD EDITION*

**Thomas Paine** (1737–1809) was a writer and a patriot during the Revolutionary War. He got his start editing *Pennsylvania Magazine*, but became famous for his pamphlet titled *Common Sense*. After the war ended, he spent some time in Europe, arguing for democratically elected governments and against monarchies. His *The Rights of Man* got him kicked out of England (where there was a king), but the French welcomed him to their country, agreeing so deeply with his philosophies of government that they made him a French citizen. When the French started beheading people during their revolution, though, he spoke out against it, to which they didn't take too kindly. Paine became quite the pain for many Europeans and Americans when his next book, *The Age of Reason*, criticized organized religion. People stopped buying his books—they even stopped acknowledging his contributions to the American Revolution—and he was poor for the rest of his life.

# THE DECLARATION OF INDEPENDENCE

**Thomas Jefferson** (1743–1826) was the third president of the United States, but long before his election he was a writer arguing for his country's independence. When the Continental Congress gathered a committee to draft the Declaration of Independence, Jefferson was singled out to be its author. He'd written successfully about the reasons for revolution before (in his "Summary View of the Rights of British America") and was a natural born leader. Plus, he'd read just about everything ever published and so was able to borrow some ideas from other countries, governments, and people.

After America gained its independence, Jefferson had several jobs before winning the presidential election. He was the minister to France, the governor of Virginia, the first Secretary of State the United States ever had, the founder of the University of Virginia, and the vice president under John Adams. As president, he made the Louisiana Purchase and then sent Lewis and Clark out on their expedition. The letters that he and John Adams exchanged were collected and published and still stand today as a great source of information about the formation and development of our country.

# PREAMBLE TO THE U.S. CONSTITUTION

**Gouverneur Morris** was a statesman from New York. He helped author the state constitution at the age of 25! After moving to Philadelphia, the people of Pennsylvania elected Morris to the Constitutional Convention in 1787. He served on the "Committee of Stile and Arrangement" that gets credit for writing all of the articles and clauses of the U.S. Constitution. Proof of Morris's role came from the biography of Madison, who said that "The finish given to the style and arrangement of the Constitution fairly belongs to the pen of Mr. Morris" and that "the entire text of the preamble and most of the stylistic improvements to the Constitution came from Morris' pen." Sounds like Madison really respected Morris's pen!

Madison is a reliable witness as history has long credited him with being the "architect" of the Constitution. If you think about it, it only makes sense that no one person be called its author as the document was supposed to be drawn up, edited, and ratified by a convention of representatives. Still, the truth about Morris writing the Preamble and about Madison's important role eventually became common knowledge. Morris returned to New York and was elected to Congress in 1800. It's fitting that he served in the senate because the idea of giving all states equal representation (two senators per state) was largely his.

# THE BILL OF RIGHTS

The Virginia Declaration of Rights was written by **George Mason** (1725–1792) and ratified in 1776, right before Mason left to attend the Continental Congress. Not only did his work in Virginia have an influence on Thomas Jefferson's Declaration of Independence, it had a direct effect on the Bill of Rights, which, you'll remember, are the first 10 amendments to the Constitution.

Mason didn't sign the first draft of the constitution that was sent around for state approval because it didn't include amendments to protect state and individual rights. Mason was worried about the federal government having too much power, so he refused to vote for it. His home state of Virginia agreed, and when they sent in their proposal for improving the constitution (essentially stating what it would take for them to ratify it), the model of the amendments was Mason's Declaration of Rights. This is why Mason is generally acknowledged as the author of the Bill of Rights and why it's important to recognize that Mason was one of our most important Founding Fathers.

# EXCERPT FROM *MARBURY V. MADISON*

**John Marshall** (1755–1835) was the chief justice of the Supreme Court when the case of *Marbury v. Madison* was heard. He was the fourth chief justice in the country's short history, but he had the greatest impact, helping to establish the court as a legitimate branch of the federal government. His idea of judicial review, which allows the Supreme Court to strike down laws that violate the Constitution, gave the court this level of legitimacy.

Marshall fought in the Revolutionary War and served in the House of Representatives. He was a Federalist, in favor of a strong national government, and so was in opposition to Thomas Jefferson who was a defender of states' rights and who was unhappy with the *Marbury v. Madison* decision as he felt it gave the Supreme Court too much power. Marshall stuck to his guns, though, and as the longest-serving chief justice in Supreme Court history he remained a Federalist throughout. It is said that the Constitution as it's known today is the one that Marshall interpreted; the one that gives the federal government extensive power and that allows judicial review. *Marbury v. Madison* is just one of the cases stamped by Marshall's beliefs. Throughout his long career, he exercised the Supreme Court's power in more than 1,000 cases!

# "THE STAR-SPANGLED BANNER"

When first written, "The Star-Spangled Banner" was a poem and not a song, and it was written by a lawyer and not a poet! Regardless, **Francis Scott Key** (1779–1843) gets the credit for writing the words that were eventually set to music and later named our national anthem. For his efforts, Key was given a place in the Songwriter's Hall of Fame and in just about every American history book ever written. For many years after the war ended, Key served as the district attorney of Washington, DC.

One interesting note from Key's law career is that he defended Sam Houston, who'd attacked another Congressman, during a famous trial in the House of Representatives. Another fact you might not know is that Key was related to Francis Scott Key Fitzgerald, better known as F. Scott Fitzgerald and the author of *The Great Gatsby*.

# EXCERPT FROM THE MONROE DOCTRINE

The Monroe Doctrine has two authors, really: the president, **James Monroe** (1758–1831), and his secretary of state, **John Quincy Adams** (1767–1848). Adams basically wrote the first draft of Monroe's speech to Congress, but he'd contributed greatly to the policy even before then. Not only did Adams help to develop these protectionist ideas, he convinced Monroe to declare them as America's policy rather than simply signing on as Great Britain's ally and following their lead. The United States was still establishing itself as a world power and this simple gesture aided in that cause.

Before becoming the fifth president of the United States, Monroe fought in the Revolutionary War and then practiced law in Virginia. He served on the Continental Congress and as a senator in the U.S. Congress. As if this isn't enough, he was also the governor of Virginia and a secretary of state. In addition to defending the United States and its neighbors against European interference with his doctrine, Monroe welcomed five states (Mississippi, Illinois, Alabama, Maine, and Missouri) into the union. Adams, the son of a president, succeeded Monroe as the sixth president and served four years. By following Monroe, he ensured that the Monroe Doctrine would be carried out as he'd originally intended. After leaving office, Adams enjoyed continued fame as a lawyer, including successfully defending the Africans from the slave ship Amistad.

# SOJOURNER TRUTH'S "AIN'T I A WOMAN?" SPEECH

**Sojourner Truth** (ca. 1797–1883) was born into slavery—thus the question about her exact birth date, circa 1797—but gained her freedom through New York's Emancipation Act in 1827. When she began to tour the nation, speaking in favor of religion and women's rights and against slavery, she took the name Sojourner Truth. It's interesting to note that Truth had three names during her life. She was born Isabella Baumfree, later took the last name of her slave master (Van Wagener), and finally, in 1843, adopted the name Sojourner Truth. To sojourn is to rest, but for the rest of her life Sojourner Truth refused to rest, traveling and speaking the truth before large audiences wherever she went.

She needed help writing her popular autobiography, *Narrative of Sojourner Truth*, because she could not read or write. What she could do was inspire people with her words. Truth spoke so well that in 1864, Abraham Lincoln invited her to the White House. She continued to tour until the day she died, but as time passed she shifted more of her focus toward women's suffrage (the right to vote).

# THE EMANCIPATION PROCLAMATION AND GETTYSBURG ADDRESS

**Abraham Lincoln** (1809–1865) was the 16th president of the United States and is considered to be one of our country's greatest. Of the many things he did well, debating and giving speeches were among the top. Not only could he hold his audience's attention with his skills of public speaking, his writing was superb. Brief and to the point! His writing was so good, in fact, that he's the only person to have two historical documents featured in this book. The Emancipation Proclamation shows not only Lincoln's writing skills but also his political savvy, while the Gettysburg Address is an example of his writing and speech-making abilities all wrapped into one.

A self-educated man and a lawyer by trade, Lincoln served in the Illinois legislature before running for U.S. Senate in 1958. One interesting fact is that he lost this race yet, two years later, was elected president! The Civil War began soon after his inauguration and unfortunately, five days after war's end, in April of 1865, he was assassinated.

# EXCERPT FROM MARK TWAIN'S
# *THE ADVENTURES OF HUCKLEBERRY FINN*

**Samuel Clemens** (1835–1910) began writing under the name
Mark Twain in 1863 when he signed an article about his travels with
that name. Mark Twain is a boating term that means "two fathoms
deep," which is a warning to steamboat pilots as it means there's shal-
low water. Twain learned this term as he worked the Mississippi River,
the setting of his most famous novel, *The Adventures of Huckleberry
Finn*. Twain's first published writing appeared mostly in newspapers
and consisted of reports he made about his travels: everywhere from
Nevada to California to Hawaii.

In 1876, 100 years after America declared her independence, Twain
published *The Adventures of Tom Sawyer*, the book that introduced
Huck Finn to the world. In 1884, that character got his own novel and
as is rarely the case with a sequel, far surpassed the original. Twain
wrote books until the day he died, but his legacy as one of America's
finest writers was cemented by *The Adventures of Huckleberry Finn*.

# EXCERPT FROM UPTON SINCLAIR'S *THE JUNGLE*

**Upton Sinclair** (1878–1968) earned his first money from writing at the age of 15. Ironically, he had to finance his most famous book, paying for *The Jungle* himself after a couple of publishers rejected it. You just know they were kicking themselves when they saw how much Sinclair earned on it! With the money he made, Sinclair tried to open a Socialist colony (a place where everything is owned and operated cooperatively by a group of people) in New Jersey, but it was destroyed by a fire.

Sinclair continued to write and in 1942 won a Pulitzer Prize for his novel, *Dragon's Teeth*, which is about the rise of the Nazi Party. He ran for governor of California as a Socialist, but lost. He released an autobiography in 1962 and despite writing almost 100 books will always be remembered for *The Jungle* and the way it led to passage of the Pure Food and Drugs Act and Meat Inspection Act in 1906.

# EXCERPT FROM
# *BROWN V. BOARD OF EDUCATION*

Before becoming chief justice of the Supreme Court, **Earl Warren** (1891–1974) was a district attorney in California who made a name for himself by making sure that each of the accused he was trying to convict had a publicly appointed attorney. (It's now a law that the court will assign an attorney if a defendant can't afford one.) It was in California that Warren was first exposed to racism, but there are two details about this that you might not expect: (1) this racism was anti-Asian and not anti-black, and (2) during World War II, when he was the attorney general of California, Warren supported removing all people of Japanese ancestry to internment camps. This, in turn, helped him to win the election for governor, but he would later write about how deeply he regretted taking this stance and being partially responsible for this upheaval of so many American citizens. With future decisions, he proved himself to be more sensitive toward race issues, especially in his *Brown v. Board of Education* ruling.

Under Warren, the Supreme Court defended the idea that the Constitution requires the U.S. government to act fairly toward all individuals. "Civil rights" is another way of saying "individual rights," and protecting individuals was certainly Warren's priority. He lost in a bid to be the president, and the nation is almost better off, considering how much he was able to accomplish as chief justice.

# PRESIDENT JOHN F. KENNEDY'S INAUGURAL ADDRESS

**John F. Kennedy** (1917–1963), the 35th president of the United States, gets sole credit for writing his inauguration speech and for most of his other speeches, despite the advice he got from friends, aides, and clergymen. In those speeches, as well as his book, *Profiles in Courage*, Kennedy proved himself to be one of the most quotable presidents ever.

Kennedy was assassinated while in office, but before his election he had a pretty amazing life. The Kennedy family was already well known for its wealth and involvement in politics, and Kennedy was the hope of the family. His younger brother Bobby had political aspirations but, sadly, was also assassinated. President Kennedy served during World War II, and then he represented Massachusetts in Congress for 13 years before his election. It was in 1960 that the first televised debate was held, and the fact that Kennedy appeared much more calm, and much more handsome, than opponent Richard Nixon gave him a leg up in his campaign. His wife, Jackie (also considered a pillar of calm and confidence), stayed in the public eye for the rest of her life as did their children.

# PRESIDENT RONALD REAGAN'S REMARKS AT THE BRANDENBURG GATE

**Ronald Reagan** (1911–2004) was a sports broadcaster, a famous actor, a governor of California, and finally a two-term president. Reagan will be remembered not only for his role in ending the Cold War but for his conservative economic policies and the fact that he began his political career as a Democrat before switching to the Republican Party. This contributed to the development of his deep belief in capitalism and his deep feelings against communism. Both of these opinions were obvious in his remarks at the Brandenburg Gate and in several other speeches he made during his eight years in office.

Less than 100 days after taking office, an attempt was made on Reagan's life, but fortunately he survived. He was known for his love of jelly beans, and a Gallop Poll found him to be the most popular president ever. Finally, it should be no surprise that he's included in this book because his nickname was "The Great Communicator."